DESSERTS
with Schmecks Appeal

EDNA STAEBLER

McGraw-Hill Ryerson
Toronto   Montreal

McClelland & Stewart
Toronto

Desserts with Schmecks Appeal

© 1991 by Edna Staebler

All rights reserved. No part of this publication may be reproduced or transmitted in any form or by any means, or stored in a data base and retrieval system, without the prior written permission of the publisher.

First published in 1991 by

MCGRAW-HILL RYERSON LIMITED
300 Water Street
Whitby, Canada
LlN 9B6

MCCLELLAND & STEWART LIMITED
481 University Avenue
Toronto, Canada
M5G 2E9

1 2 3 4 5 6 7 8 9 10 W 0 9 8 7 6 5 4 3 2 1

ISBN: 0-7700-8271-0

Canadian Cataloguing in Publication Data

Staebler, Edna, date
  Desserts with schmecks appeal

(Schmecks appeal cookbook series)
ISBN 0-7710-8271-1

1. Desserts.   2. Cookery, Mennonite.   3. Cookery — Ontario — Waterloo (Regional municipality).
I. Title.   II. Series: Staebler, Edna, date. The schmecks appeal cookbook series.

TX773.S85 1991   641.8'6   C90-095546-5

Printed and bound in Canada

CONTENTS

DESSERTS   1

APPLE DESSERTS   2

FRUIT DESSERTS   13

RHUBARB DESSERTS   23

PLUM DESSERTS   30

COMPANY DESSERTS   36

RICE AND TAPIOCA PUDDINGS   52

BAKED PUDDINGS   55

GELATINE DESSERTS   61

FROZEN DESSERTS   68

STEAMED PUDDINGS   77

DESSERT SAUCES   84

INDEX   90

DESSERTS

When my two sisters and I were skinny little girls living at home, Mother never served a meal without fresh fruit for dessert in summer, bananas, and oranges, or canned fruit in winter, and always cookies or cake. Sometimes she made puddings; on Saturday and on Sunday we had pie; for company there was always a choice of fruit, cake and cookies, pie, cheese, pudding, or something soft, luscious, and loaded with calories — like maple mousse or homemade ice cream. And we didn't get fat.

The choices at Bevvy's table are no less generous. Though pie, fruit, and cake are Mennonite favourites, Bevvy's little notebook has recipes for custards, dumplings baked in brown-sugar sauce, and dozens of puddings, most of them steamed.

David and the children smile broadly when they come in from the cold on a bleak winter's day as the steamed pudding emits its fragrance of spices and fruit from the top of Bevvy's ever-burning black wood stove. Steaming for two or three hours, it gently humidifies the air as well.

Salome makes a sauce for the pudding and puts a pitcher of thick sweet cream on the table "for those who like either or both."

Lyddy goes down to the basement, brings up a jar of canned peaches and empties them into Bevvy's tall pressed-glass compote. She then cuts a cake into generous slices and puts fat molasses and date cookies on a plate.

"I feel real bad that we haven't got pie yet," Bevvy apologizes to me, "but sometimes, like now at the end of the week, they are all gone: and I just stir up a pudding."

I assure her that, because of the calories, I sometimes don't have any dessert at all.

"Ach no!" she exclaims in amazement. "Without dessert at the back part of a meal we'd feel we weren't finished."

Amsey says, "We would all get up from the table starving to death."

APPLE DESSERTS

Apples no doubt make the most popular of all fruit desserts because they are so versatile and obtainable, from the best applesauce-making apples that ripen late in July to different varieties of fall apples, and winter apples that can be kept in a cool place until spring.

If you want to please your family, yourself, and your friends, make them an apple cobbler, apfelstrudel, apple dumplings, puddings, and several kinds of schnitz pies (see Pies and Tarts with Schmecks Appeal). Apple desserts will make you happy and healthy.

APPLESAUCE

The moment the first green Harvest apples appear at the market I buy a six-quart basket of them and immediately make the most wonderful applesauce in the world.

I wash the **apples**, cut out the blossom ends and stems, cut the apples into quarters and plunge them into boiling water in a big kettle — enough water to cover three-quarters of the apples. Boil the apples till they are soft, puffy, and their skins have fallen off; stir them occasionally so the top ones will go down to the bottom and they'll all cook evenly. While it is hot, put the whole mass through a food mill or colander to remove the skins, cores, and seeds. Or whirl in a food processor until smooth, then strain to get rid of the bits of core that look like fingernail parings. Then while still piping hot, add **sugar** — about 1 cup to every 2 quarts of applesauce — more if the apples are very sour (taste till it seems just right — not too sweet). Sprinkle liberally with **cinnamon**, cool it, then try to find enough covered containers and enough space in your fridge to keep it — it's too good to be kept very long. (By boiling the applesauce after you put in the sugar and cinnamon and then pouring it into sterilized jars, you can keep it as you would any canned fruit — but I don't think it tastes as good.)

I like this Harvest or Yellow Transparent applesauce to be quite thin and cold. I'll eat it every day till it's all gone. With toasted homemade bread in the morning, and as a dessert with a nut loaf, gingerbread, molasses, or oatmeal cookies it can't be beat.

My sister Norm doesn't like my applesauce; she says it's too thin. She and Ralph like theirs almost thick enough to be eaten with a fork. If you like it that way, use just enough water to cover the bottom layer of apples in the kettle.

AUNTIE'S APPLE DUMPLINGS

When Mother made apple dumplings, we didn't want anything else for supper.

2 cups flour
2 teaspoons baking powder
1 teaspoon salt
⅔ cup shortening
½ cup milk
5 apples, peeled, cored, and cut in half
3 tablespoons sugar
½ teaspoon cinnamon

Sauce:
2 cups brown sugar
2 cups water
¼ cup butter
¼ teaspoon cinnamon or nutmeg

Sift together the flour, baking powder, and salt; cut in the shortening until the mixture is crumbly. Add the milk and mix just enough to hold the dough together. Pat the dough into a ball, put it on a floured surface and roll it till it is about ¼ inch thick. Cut the rolled dough into 10 square pieces, each large enough to cover half an apple. Place apple halves on squares. Fill the cavities in the apples with the sugar and cinnamon mixed together. Bring the corners of the squares of dough to the centre top and pinch them and the sides together to cover the apple completely. Put the apples an inch apart in a buttered baking pan and pour the sauce over them. To make the sauce: simply combine all the ingredients and pour over the dumplings in the pan. Bake at 375°F for about 40 minutes. Have a look before that. Serve the dumplings hot with whole milk or cream poured over them if you think it necessary.

APPLE OATMEAL SQUARES

All winter I like to keep apples in my cold room. With a good stock of apple recipes, I'm never without the makings of a dessert. These can be put together in a hurry, and they taste good even a day or two later.

Crumbs:
1 cup flour
½ teaspoon baking soda
½ teaspoon salt
½ cup brown sugar
1 cup rolled oats
½ cup shortening

Filling:
4 cups sliced apples
2 tablespoons butter
½ cup sugar
Cinnamon

Mix the dry ingredients for crumbs; cut in the shortening till crumbly. Spread half the mixture in buttered 9" x 9" pan. Spread the apples over the crumbs, dot with butter, and sprinkle with sugar. Cover with the remaining crumbs and sprinkle cinnamon over all. Bake at 350°F for about 40 minutes, or until top is golden and the apples are tender. Cut in squares and serve warm.

GERMAN APFEL PFANNKUCHEN
(Apple Pancake)

This attractive, flat, apple-custard pancake is a not-so-sweet dessert to be served with cheese or syrup or ice cream. Easy to make and serve.

4 eggs
½ cup flour
½ teaspoon salt
¼ cup sugar
½ cup milk
½ teaspoon grated lemon rind
1 tablespoon lemon juice
1 apple, cored and coarsely grated
2 tablespoons butter

Beat eggs until light. Sift together flour, salt, and sugar; add alternately with the milk to the beaten eggs. Mix well, then stir in the lemon rind and juice. Fold in the grated apple. Melt the butter in a 10-inch skillet. Pour in the batter and bake at 350°F for 30 minutes, or until set. Loosen the sides and bottom of the pancake and serve at once.

Choosing Recipes

When I look through my cookbooks for recipes, I always skip all those that have long lists of ingredients. Not because they wouldn't be good, but because I can't be bothered with anything that isn't quick and easy to make. I like recipes that use ingredients that I have in my cupboard or fridge — unless I am about to splurge and go into town to shop for something special. But that doesn't happen often because most of my invitations are given at the last minute when I happen to feel like having someone to eat with.

Once I invited two couples for dinner but they couldn't come for two weeks — and for two weeks I worried about what I would feed them. I had such a long time to be prepared that I had no excuse if everything wasn't perfect.

APFELSTRUDEL

A German specialty, often served in Kitchener and Waterloo, it has many variations — some of them pretty dull and dry. I'll never forget the Apfelstrudel a German woman served me warm from the oven; she told me how to make it.

2½ cups flour
1 teaspoon salt
2 tablespoons shortening
2 eggs, lightly beaten
½ cup warm water
⅓ cup melted butter
5 cups sliced apples
½ cup seedless raisins
1 cup brown sugar
½ cup chopped nuts
½ teaspoon cinnamon
Grated rind of 1 lemon

Sift the flour and salt together. Cut in the shortening and add the eggs and water. Knead well, then throw or beat the dough against a board until it blisters. Stand the dough in a warm place under a cloth for 20 minutes. Cover the kitchen table with a small white cloth and flour it. Put the dough in the center of it and roll to ⅛" thickness then pull it out with your hands very carefully to the thickness of tissue paper. Brush the dough with melted butter then spread with a mixture of the fruits, sugar, nuts, cinnamon, and lemon rind. Fold in the outer edges of the dough and roll like a jelly roll about 4 inches wide. Bake in a 450°F oven for 10 minutes, reduce the heat to 400°F and bake about 20 minutes longer. Let it cool. Cut in slices about two inches wide. It should be flaky, moist, and one of the best things you've ever tasted.

GRANDMOTHER'S CROWNEST

An upside-down apple pudding. Martina Schneiker says this was her husband's favourite dessert.

12 medium apples
1 cup sugar

Batter:
1 cup flour
3 tablespoons sugar
1 teaspoon baking powder
½ teaspoon salt
3 heaping tablespoons shortening
¼ cup milk

Topping:
1 pint whipping cream
1 teaspoon sugar
Cinnamon

Core and slice the apples, stir in the 1 cup sugar and pour into a buttered 9" x 13" pan. Sift the flour with 3 tablespoons sugar, baking powder, and salt; blend in the shortening. Pour in the milk and mix until the right consistency for rolling. Roll out the dough to cover the apples in the pan, venting the top. Bake at 350°F for 35 minutes. Cool completely. When ready to serve, invert on a platter, giving it a quick flip. Cover with sweetened whipped cream and a sprinkle of cinnamon.

HASTY APPLE PUDDING

This is a light, tasty pudding with a crisp meringue-like top.

Filling:
**4 cups sliced apples
2 tablespoons sugar
½ teaspoon cinnamon
¼ teaspoon nutmeg
2 tablespoons butter
¼ cup hot water**

Batter:
**2 eggs
1 cup sugar
¼ cup melted butter
⅔ cup flour
2 teaspoons baking powder
½ teaspoon salt**

Spread the sliced apples into a buttered 9" x 9" baking dish. Blend the sugar, cinnamon, and nutmeg; sprinkle over the apples. Melt the butter in the hot water and pour over the apples. To make the batter, beat eggs. Add the sugar and keep on beating. Then beat in the melted butter. Add the flour, baking powder, and salt, beating until smooth. Spread evenly over the apples in the baking dish. Bake at 350°F for 30 minutes or until apples are soft and top is brown. Serve warm or cold.

APPLE SPONGE PUDDING

From Eliza Gingerich's grandmother, handed down because it's so good.

    6 medium-sized apples
    2 eggs, separated
    1 cup white sugar
    1 cup flour
    1 teaspoon baking powder
    ½ teaspoon salt
    1 cup water
    1 teaspoon vanilla
    ¼ cup butter
    2 cups brown sugar

Peel and slice the apples. Beat the egg yolks, add the white sugar and beat until light. Sift the flour, baking powder, and salt together, and add alternately with the water and vanilla to the sugar-egg mixture. Fold in the stiffly beaten egg whites.

In a baking dish, melt the butter and brown sugar; spread the sliced apples over the mixture. Pour the batter over the apples and bake at 350°F for about 45 minutes. Serve warm with whipped or ice cream.

This should serve eight people but it probably won't.

FRUITY APPLE PUDDING

Fresh and fruity in a mince-pie sort of way, this can be eaten hot or cold.

    1 cup butter
    3 cups flour
    2 egg yolks or 1 egg
    ¼ cup cold water
    Juice and grated rind of 1 lemon
    ¼ cup sugar

Blend the butter and flour. Beat the egg yolks and add the water to them. Combine the mixtures, adding juice, grated lemon rind, and sugar. Pat two-thirds of the dough into a 9" x 9" baking dish.

> **2 quarts apples, diced**
> **1 cup sugar**
> **1 cup seeded raisins**
> **½ cup currants**
> **¼ cup almonds, blanched and chopped**
> **¼ cup red or white sweet wine**
> **Juice and grated rind of 1 lemon**

Mix these ingredients and pour onto dough in baking dish; criss-cross remaining dough over the top. Bake 50 to 60 minutes at 400°F.

SPEEDY APPLE NUT PUDDING

It didn't take longer than twelve minutes to get this dessert into the oven on the day my publisher, Jack McClelland, called to say he'd be coming from Toronto in time for lunch. The pudding turned out well and Jack had two helpings.

> **1 egg**
> **¾ cup white or brown sugar**
> **½ teaspoon salt**
> **½ cup flour**
> **1 teaspoon baking powder**
> **1½ cups chopped apples, not peeled**
> **¾ cup finely chopped nuts**

Beat the egg, pour in the sugar and salt and beat together. By hand, stir in the flour and baking powder sifted together. Stir in the apples and nuts. Spread in a buttered 9-inch pie plate or a square cake pan, if you'd rather serve squares than wedges. Bake in a 325°F oven for about 35 to 40 minutes. Serve hot or cold with whipped cream or ice cream.

APPLE BETTY

You just can't beat an Apple Betty. At the bottom of this recipe someone named George wrote, "Undoubtedly delicious."

> ¾ cup sugar
> 1 tablespoon flour
> 1 teaspoon cinnamon
> 4 cups sliced apples, not peeled
>
> *Topping:*
> 1 cup rolled oats or wheat flakes
> ½ cup brown sugar
> ½ cup flour
> ¼ teaspoon baking soda
> ¼ teaspoon baking powder
> ¼ cup melted butter

Blend sugar, flour, and cinnamon, then stir the mixture into the apples in a buttered baking dish. Combine the rolled oats, brown sugar, flour, baking soda, and baking powder with the melted butter to make crumbs. Pour the crumbs over the apple mixture in the casserole and bake at 375°F for 35 to 40 minutes. Serve hot or cold with whipped or vanilla ice cream. You'll find out George wasn't wrong.

FRUIT DESSERTS

One day in August I had dinner with a friend who served imported California seedless grapes for dessert. Can you imagine that? When the Kitchener and Waterloo markets were teeming with homegrown peaches, plums, apricots, apples, pears, cantaloupes, and grapes in all their glorious splendour.

STRAWBERRY OR PEACH SHORTCAKE

Years ago I should have mimeographed copies of this old-fashioned biscuit-dough shortcake recipe — it would have saved me the time I've spent giving it to all the people who've eaten it at my table.

4 cups flour
1 cup sugar
2 tablespoons baking powder
1 teaspoon baking soda
1 teaspoon salt
1 cup shortening
2 cups buttermilk

Mix the dry ingredients and the shortening till the mixture is crumbly. Add the milk and mix just enough to make sure the dry part is moistened. Spread the dough out in a greased cake pan — quite a large flat one — or you can use half the recipe and put the batter into a 9" x 9" one. Sprinkle white sugar over the top and bake in a 400°F oven for about 20 minutes, or a bit longer — prick the centre to be sure. Serve warm and smothered with sugared berries or sliced peaches. You don't need to split it and butter it or slather it with whipped cream. This one stands on its own.

GLOWING CHERRY BETTY

Loaded with nourishment, you won't have to force anyone to eat this. Try it with various fruits.

Stir together in a bowl:

> **2 cups pitted cherries, frozen or fresh, with their juice**
> **½ cup white or brown sugar mixed with**
> **3 tablespoons flour**
> **½ teaspoon almond flavouring**

Turn the mixture into a buttered 9" x 9" cake pan.

> **1 cup shelled, toasted sunflower seeds**
> **½ cup rolled oats**
> **½ cup whole-wheat flour**
> **½ cup wheat germ**
> **¼ cup brown sugar or honey**
> **4 tablespoons butter or margarine**

Mix topping ingredients well and sprinkle over the cherry mixture. Bake at 350°F for 45 to 50 minutes. Serve hot or cold with cream, whipped cream, or ice cream.

COUSIN LUCY'S MERINGUE PEACH PIE

When we ate this at Cousin Lucy's place in Grand Rapids, Michigan, we thought it was the most delicious thing we had ever tasted in all our lives. (I was fourteen.) I still think it's one of the most glamorous party desserts to be made throughout the fresh fruit season. If you have an electric mixer, it's a cinch; Cousin Lucy had to beat the eggs with a wire whisk. Try it with fresh strawberries or raspberries too.

4 egg whites
¼ teaspoon cream of tartar
½ teaspoon salt
1 cup sugar

In a large bowl, let the egg whites warm to room temperature. Beat the egg whites with the cream of tartar and salt until they are stiff, but not stiff enough to form peaks. Gradually beat in the sugar a bit at a time and keep on beating and beating until the meringue is very firm and the peaks very stiff, shiny, and moist. Spread the meringue over the bottom of the large, well-greased pie plate, about ¼ of an inch thick; cover the sides an inch deep and as high as the meringue will stay. Bake at 275°F for an hour — it should be light beige and crisp. Don't put it too near the floor of the oven or its bottom might burn. When it is cold — and you can keep the baked meringue for several days — fill the hollow of the pie shell with about ¾ of an inch of **ice cream**. Over that, and nicely filling the whole thing, pour in coarsely sliced and **lightly sugared peaches — or strawberries, or raspberries**.

This one is really ambrosial. And what are you going to do with those egg yolks? Make a sponge cake, or noodles, or custard sauce — or simply lose them in an omelette or scrambled eggs.

FRUIT ROLL

Fruit rolled in a fluffy biscuit blanket baked in syrup. Try it with rhubarb, or strawberries, raspberries, peaches, apples, raisins, any other fruit you fancy.

Syrup:
2 cups water
1½ cups brown sugar
Butter the size of an egg

Biscuit dough:
2 cups flour
2 tablespoons sugar
1 tablespoon baking powder
1 teaspoon salt
⅓ cup shortening
⅔ cup milk, or more

Filling:
3 tablespoons softened butter
½ cup brown sugar
3 cups cubed fruit (fresh or frozen)
½ teaspoon cinnamon (optional)

Blend the syrup ingredients in a 9" x 13" baking pan and put it in the oven while it is heating to 400°F. Meantime sift the dry ingredients for the biscuit dough; cut in the shortening till fine, stir in the milk to make a soft dough. Roll the dough ⅛ inch thick into an oblong about 12" x 6" and spread with the filling. Roll like a jelly roll, pinch the edges to seal. Slice 1½ inches thick and place the slices cut-side-down in the pan of boiling syrup, or lay the entire roll in the hot syrup in the baking pan. Bake the cut rolls in a 400°F oven for about 20 minutes, 30 to 40 for the uncut version. Serve warm.

EVA'S MINCE MEAT ROLLS

Instead of the fruit filling Eva spreads the dough with **1½ cups prepared mince meat**, makes the syrup in a saucepan, and pours the hot syrup over the rolls at the table.

FLAMING PEAR MELBA

When my neighbour Laurie Bennett entertains, she likes to serve classy desserts. This one was impressive on a snowy February night.

   1 can pear halves
   1 4-ounce package cream cheese
   1 tablespoon sugar
   1 10-ounce package frozen raspberries, thawed
   1 tablespoon cornstarch
   ¼ cup sugar
   ¼ cup brandy

Drain the pear halves well, reserving syrup. Blend the cream cheese with the 1 tablespoon sugar and enough of the pear syrup to make a smooth paste. Using about a tablespoon of the cheese mixture at a time, stick the pear halves together, then refrigerate. Meanwhile, heat the raspberries, then strain out the seeds. Blend the raspberry juice, cornstarch, and the ¼ cup sugar; stir over medium heat until thick, adding a bit of the pear syrup if you like. Pour the hot sauce over the cold pears in a crockery bowl. Heat the brandy, pour it over the pears, and set it alight. Serve the pears in champagne glasses. That is class!

RASPBERRY PUDDING

A company dish, sweet and pretty, with a crisp, almost meringue-like top covering the moist goodies underneath. It can be made with a variety of fruits.

Fruit:
2 or 3 cups raspberries (or 1 package frozen)
2 tablespoons flour
2 tablespoons sugar
2 tablespoons butter

Topping:
⅓ cup butter
2 cups sugar
1 egg
1 cup flour
1 teaspoon baking powder
½ teaspoon salt
⅓ cup milk

Spread the fruit on the bottom on a 9" x 9" buttered and floured cake pan — preferably Pyrex. Sprinkle flour and sugar over the fruit. (If you use frozen fruit, let it thaw first and blend the juice with the sugar and flour before pouring it over the fruit in the pan.) Cut the butter over the fruit in paper-thin slices.

Now, in a bowl, cream the butter and sugar; blend in the egg; sift the flour, baking powder, and salt and add to the creamed mixture alternately with the milk. Beat well. Drop the batter in spoonfuls over the fruit. Bake at 350°F for about half an hour — longer if you used frozen berries. Serve warm or cold with whipped or ice cream, topping with a few whole, especially nice berries. And be prepared to hand out the recipe.

FRESH STRAWBERRIES, LEMON, AND WINE

At dinner one May night in Italy, we were appalled to see our waiter sprinkle perfect, ripe strawberries with sugar, then lemon juice. But when we ate, we found that the strawberry flavour had been heightened by the lemon. Try this with your strawberry shortcake — or strawberries served alone: from **2 quarts of berries** pick out the most perfect ones, sprinkle with sugar; mash the imperfect berries with the juice of a small **lemon** — or half a lemon — slightly less than ½ cup sugar and add **1 cup light sweet red wine**. Pour this purée over the whole berries, stir well together and serve with the shortcake or in a dish with scones or cake on the side. Use raspberries in the same way.

To Plan A Meal

This is the way to do it. Sit down with a pencil and paper and dream about it, put down everything you can think of that you are going to need for your table and your menu. On another paper put everything you need to shop for. This planning could take quite a lot of enjoyable sitting and relaxing time. When you have finished, you'll feel you are well on your way; you couldn't possibly flub it because it's all there; you just have to follow the blueprint. If the meal is a success, save the menu to use another time, but note who your guests were so you won't repeat the meal when they come again.

If you're planning a party or even entertaining a few, you're going to have to go out to shop. You just can't give them limp lettuce and tired fruit. So while you're about it, you might as well plan to splurge; pick up the few extras that you don't usually have in your pantry. Now is the time for experimentation. Now you can make that fancy dessert that you wouldn't dare to eat by yourself.

FRESH WINTER FRUIT

All my life I've been eating this fresh winter fruit and I've never tired of having it several times in a week — with various cookies or cake. It's so simple; all you do is cut up oranges, grapefruit, slice a banana, slice an apple or two, cut up a few maraschino cherries for colour if you like, grape halves and pineapple chunks. Sometimes my combination of fruits has been limited to just bananas and oranges.

After cutting, I mix them in a bowl, sprinkle them with sugar and serve. If I want to be a bit more subtle — and to create more juice — I add a tablespoonful or two, or more, of muscatel, sherry, or apricot brandy.

PRUNE WHIP

We never wanted plain prunes again after Mother had treated us to this.

- **3 egg whites**
- **¼ teaspoon salt**
- **½ cup sugar**
- **2 tablespoons lemon juice**
- **2 cups finely chopped cooked prunes**

Beat the egg whites with salt until stiff but not dry. Add the sugar gradually, beating it in. Add the lemon juice to the prune pulp and gradually beat it into the egg mixture until the whole thing is fluffy. Pile lightly into individual serving dishes and chill.

Or pour into a greased baking dish, set in a pan of water and bake at 325°F until it is firm.

Serve with whipped cream or Custard Sauce (page 85).

Other fruits may be used instead of the prunes — apricots, peaches, strawberries, bananas — but not baked.

SPICY DRIED FRUIT

Every morning for breakfast at Bevvy Martin's farmhouse, we had *schnitz und gwetcha* (dried apples and prunes). This dessert might be a good innovation.

**½ cup prunes
¾ cup dried apricots
¾ cup raisins
⅔ cup sugar
1 thin strip lemon rind
1 teaspoon allspice
1 teaspoon nutmeg
1-inch piece cinnamon stick
Sour cream**

Put prunes, apricots, and raisins in a bowl. Add enough boiling water to cover and leave overnight. Next day, drain. Put fruit into a saucepan with sugar, lemon rind, spices, and enough water to cover. Put a lid on the pan and simmer gently until fruit is tender. Cool and remove lemon rind and cinnamon stick. Put fruit into a serving bowl and chill thoroughly. Serve with a bowl of sour cream to spoon on top of each serving.

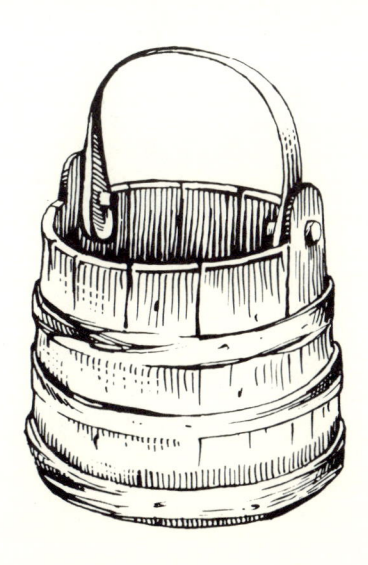

EVA'S FRUIT BATTER PUDDING

Made with fresh or frozen or soaked dried fruit, whatever you happen to have.

> 2 cups or more sweetened fruit
> 3 tablespoons butter
> ⅓ cup sugar
> 1 egg
> 1 cup flour
> 1½ teaspoons baking powder
> ¾ cup milk
> ¼ teaspoon salt
> ½ teaspoon almond flavouring

In a buttered baking dish, Eva puts at least 2 cupfuls of fruit, usually more, with sugar to taste. Over it she pours the batter, mixed in the order given. She bakes it at 350°F for about half an hour. Serves it with whipped or ice cream, or just so.

WATERMELON BOAT

The day Dorothy Cressman came to our Book Group's annual pot-luck supper carrying a scooped-out half watermelon filled with balls of cantaloupe, honey dew melon, watermelon, pineapple pieces, strawberries, and green seedless grapes, with mint sprigs, we all cheered at the sight. And the refreshing taste was as good as the look.

RHUBARB DESSERTS

There probably isn't a garden in Canada that doesn't have a patch of rhubarb tucked away in a corner, yet when I went through dozens of cookbooks looking for rhubarb dessert recipes I found only a few. I persisted in my search and asked for rhubarb recipes from all my friends and relatives wherever I went. I finally accumulated more than one hundred recipes, more than enough for a whole chapter in my book Schmecks Appeal. *I tried and found successful ways to make rhubarb relish, salad, jelly, cobbler, conserve, punch, muffins, juice, cake, crumble, soup, bread, crunch, and whip. And at least sixty pie recipes.*

My mother was the only person I knew who enjoyed eating raw rhubarb. She'd take a fat, rosy stalk, dip the end in sugar, bite it off, and eat it without screwing up her face (which I did when I tried it). Every time she made rhubarb pie, she'd eat one stalk raw.

Rhubarb retains its freshness in the freezer more successfully than any other fruit. After it is cooked or baked, it tastes exactly as it does when taken fresh from the garden. You can use it throughout the year and imagine it is spring. Don't thaw it first.

RHUBARB CRUNCH

This is my absolute favourite — scrumptious, rich, and fail-proof. I took it to a University Women's Club pot-luck supper, and it was gone in seconds.

Crumbs:
1 cup flour
1 cup brown sugar, packed
¾ cup rolled oats
1 teaspoon salt
1 teaspoon cinnamon
½ cup melted butter

4 cups diced rhubarb

Sauce:
1 cup sugar
2 tablespoons cornstarch
1 cup water
1 teaspoon vanilla

Mix the crumb ingredients until crumbly, and press half of them in a buttered 9" x 9" baking pan. Spread the rhubarb pieces evenly over the crumbs. Combine the sauce ingredients in a saucepan and cook over moderate heat until thick and clear, then pour evenly over the rhubarb. Sprinkle the remaining crumbs over top and bake at 350°F for about 1 hour, or until golden brown. Serve warm or cold with ice cream. You'll be asked for this recipe. It's great, too, made with other fruits: apples, peaches, plums, or cherries.

RHUBARB COBBLER

Everyone loves an old-fashioned cobbler.

> 4 to 5 cups cut-up rhubarb
> Juice and grated rind of 1 orange
> 1 cup sugar
> 2 tablespoons cornstarch
> ½ cup water
>
> *Topping:*
> 1½ cups flour
> 3 teaspoons baking powder
> ½ teaspoon salt
> 3 tablespoons sugar
> 3 tablespoons shortening
> ½ cup milk

Combine the rhubarb, orange juice, rind, sugar mixed with the cornstarch, and the water; put into a 9" x 9" buttered baking dish. (If you don't have an orange, add another ½ cup water.) Bake at 350°F while you are mixing the rest. Sift together the flour, baking powder, salt, and sugar. Cut in the shortening and add enough milk to make a soft dough — without over-stirring. Spoon the dough over the rhubarb, sprinkle it with sugar, and bake at 350°F for 40 to 50 minutes, or till the cake tests done.

SPICY RHUBARB COBBLER

If you like spices, put in your preference — but not too much — with the sugar and cornstarch mixture. Try **½ teaspoon cinnamon, ¼ teaspoon nutmeg**.

RHUBARB STRAWBERRY COBBLER

Substitute strawberries for the orange or some of the rhubarb.

RHUBARB PIES

Of course, there are wonderful Rhubarb Pie recipes in another book in this series, *Pies and Tarts with Schmecks Appeal.*

BAKED RHUBARB

Bevvy says: "When the oven is hot, you might as well put in some rhubarb."

> 4 cups rhubarb, cut in 1-inch pieces
> ⅛ teaspoon salt
> ⅔ cup sugar
> ¼ teaspoon cinnamon or ginger
> 2 tablespoons water
> 2 tablespoons butter

Mix together rhubarb, salt, sugar, cinnamon, and water. Pour into a 2-quart baking dish. Dot with butter and bake, covered, at 350°F until the rhubarb is tender, about 20 minutes. Chill and serve with a plateful of oatmeal cookies, muffins, or tea biscuits.

RHUBARB DREAM

Elvina Bauman likes to make this for company. Not unlike rhubarb pie, but not as rich. Great flavour.

> *Crust:*
> 1 cup flour
> 5 tablespoons sugar
> ¼ cup butter
>
> *Topping:*
> 2 eggs
> 1½ cups sugar
> ¼ cup flour
> ¾ teaspoon salt
> 2 cups rhubarb, cut fine

Blend the crust ingredients. Press into an ungreased 9" x 9" pan. Mix topping ingredients and spoon over crust. Bake at 350°F for about 30 minutes, or until golden brown.

STEWED RHUBARB

The quickest and easiest thing to do with **rhubarb** is simply to cut it into 1-inch pieces, put it into a cooking pot with just enough **water** to cover the bottom of the pot — about ½ cup — then simmer until the rhubarb is soft. Stir in **sugar** to taste. Flavour it with **orange rind**, if you like. Cool and serve with muffins or tea biscuits as a dessert.

To make rhubarb sauce palatable with even less sugar, pour boiling water over the raw rhubarb, let stand 5 minutes, drain, then proceed as before — but use less sugar. Since strawberries are in season at the same time as spring rhubarb, you might like to put a few strawberries in the pot at the same time.

LOUISE PULKINGHORN'S RHUBARB CRISP

Norm said Louise served this dessert after dinner one night and she asked for the recipe.

4 cups chopped rhubarb
⅔ cup brown sugar
2 teaspoons grated orange rind

Topping:
½ cup brown sugar
½ cup rolled oats
1 teaspoon cinnamon
½ cup flour
⅓ cup shredded coconut
⅓ cup butter

Combine the rhubarb, sugar, and orange rind. Put in buttered 1½-quart baking dish. To make topping, combine brown sugar, rolled oats, cinnamon, flour, and coconut. Cut in butter until mixture is crumbly. Sprinkle topping evenly over rhubarb. Bake at 350°F for about 40 minutes, or until topping is brown. Serve warm with whipped cream or ice cream.

EVA'S RHUBARB CUSTARD MERINGUE

This is truly impressive and delicious.

Bottom:
1 cup flour
½ cup butter
2 tablespoons sugar
Pinch of salt

Filling:
3 egg yolks
1 cup sugar
2 tablespoons flour
Grated rind of 1 orange (optional)
½ cup milk or cream
3 cups diced rhubarb

Topping:
3 eggs whites
6 tablespoons sugar

Blend the bottom ingredients till crumbs form; press into a 9" x 9" pan and bake at 350°F for 10 minutes. Mix together all the filling ingredients in the order given. Pour over the crumb layer and bake for about half an hour. When baked, lower the oven heat to 300°F. Beat egg whites stiff with the sugar. Spread over the rhubarb and bake another 15 minutes but keep your eye on it.

AGGIE BRUBACHER'S RHUBARB ROLL

Fruit rolled in a fluffy biscuit blanket, baked in syrup. Aggie was a maid in our house when we were very young. We were always happy when Mother let her make this.

Syrup:
1½ cups sugar
2 cups water

Dough:
2 cups flour
3 teaspoons baking powder
1 teaspoon salt
⅓ cup shortening
⅔ cup milk

Filling:
3 cups cubed rhubarb (fresh or frozen)
½ cup brown sugar
3 tablespoons softened butter
½ teaspoon cinnamon

Blend the syrup ingredients in a 9" x 13" baking pan and put it in the oven while it is heating to 450°F. Sift the dry ingredients for the dough and cut in the shortening till fine. Stir in the milk to make a soft dough; roll the dough ⅛ of an inch thick into an oblong about 6" x 12". Combine filling ingredients and spread on dough. Roll like a jelly roll; pinch the edge to seal. Slice 1½ inches thick and place the slices in the pan of boiling syrup — or lay the entire roll in the hot syrup. Bake immediately at 450°F for 20 minutes for the cut roll, 30 to 40 minutes for the uncut. Serve warm with whipped or pouring cream.

RHUBARB STRAWBERRY ROLL OR TURNOVERS

Made exactly as the above Rhubarb Roll but use **1 cup strawberries** with **2 cups rhubarb**. Or you can make turnovers: cut the dough into squares and put some filling in the centre of each. Seal the edges together and place side by side in a buttered pan. Bake at 375°F for about 30 minutes.

PLUM DESSERTS

No one wonders what to do with the luscious imported red and gold plums that appear in the fruit stores at exorbitant prices. But what do you do with all those little greengages, prune plums, or navy-blue Damsons a friend has given you from a plum tree in her back yard?

Whenever I received my annual six-quart gift basket from my friend Dorothy Shoemaker's plum tree, I ate as many raw ones as my digestive system would allow, then made Plum Fool or a cobbler, and froze the rest. But what can be done with the frozen ones?

I've looked through dozens of cookbooks. Most don't mention plums. Others have perhaps one recipe; for plum tart or for Christmas plum pudding, which doesn't use any plums. Over the years, I've kept searching and asking my friends what they do with plums, till now I've collected and tried quite a number of really good recipes.

Stewed, spiced, in conserve, in chutney, or pie or cake or muffins, plums from the back yard can be a pleasant tart change of flavour for most of the year.

PARTY PLUM CAKE

This glazed dessert has a professional look but is easy to make.

>¼ cup butter
>1 cup sugar
>2 eggs, separated
>1½ cups flour
>1 teaspoon baking powder
>½ teaspoon salt
>½ cup milk
>2 cups pitted plums; blue or green —
>   but the blue are prettier

Cream together the butter, sugar, and egg yolks. Sift together the flour, baking powder, and salt; add to the creamed mixture alternately with the milk. Fold in the stiffly beaten egg whites. Pour the batter into a greased 9" x 9" cake pan, place the plums neatly on top. Sprinkle over the plums crumbs made of:

>½ cup brown sugar
>2 tablespoons flour
>1 teaspoon cinnamon
>¼ cup butter

Bake in 350°F oven for about 45 minutes. While the cake is baking, blend the glaze:

>¾ cup icing sugar
>1 tablespoon cream or milk
>½ teaspoon vanilla or almond extract

When the cake comes out of the oven, dribble the glaze generously over it. When it cools it will be shiny and handsome. Serve it warm or cold, with or without ice cream.

SAUCY PLUM PUDDING

A substantial hot pudding for a winter's night, made with the plums you froze last September. Sweet, tart, and schmecksy. If you prefer, you could make it with apples or peaches.

Sauce:
1 cup brown sugar
1 tablespoon cornstarch
2 cups water
1 tablespoon butter

Dough:
2 cups flour
½ teaspoon salt
2 teaspoons baking powder
2 tablespoons butter
1 egg
1 cup milk

Filling:
2 cups pitted and halved plums
2 tablespoons sugar

Make the sauce first. In a small saucepan, blend brown sugar and cornstarch. Pour in the water and boil for 3 minutes; stir in the butter. Then make the dough. Sift the flour, salt, and baking powder; blend in the butter. In a small bowl, beat the egg and milk together, then stir into the flour-butter mixture. Spread half the dough into a 9" x 9" pan. Place the plum halves over the dough, then sprinkle with sugar. Spread remaining dough on top. Pour the sauce over the pudding and bake at 350°F for about 30 minutes — a bit longer if your plums are still frozen. Serve hot.

PLUM COBBLER

You can make this with fresh plums, of course, but it's a great way to use your frozen ones. Butter a baking dish. Empty the frozen mass of **plums** into it. Put the dish in the oven, then turn the oven on to 350°F and let the plums thaw while you are mixing the batter. When the plums are thawed enough to break them up, stir in **sugar** and **cinnamon**.

Batter:
1½ cups flour
1 tablespoon baking powder
1 teaspoon salt
3 tablespoons butter
3 tablespoons sugar
¾ cup milk

Sift together flour, baking powder, and salt. Cream butter, sugar, and milk. Stir in the flour mixture and add enough more milk to make a soft dough. Spoon it over the sugared plums in the baking dish, then sprinkle a tablespoon of sugar over the top. Bake at 350°F for 40 to 50 minutes, or until the cake tests done and the plums are bubbling and soft. Serve warm or cold.

STEWED PLUMS

You can try all the plum recipes you like, but I don't think any of them are as good as just plain stewed plums with plain, not-too-sweet, crunchy cookies. All you need to do is halve and pit the **plums**. Put them in a saucepan with enough **water** to give them some juice and enough **sugar** to sweeten them to your taste; a sprinkling of **cinnamon or nutmeg** will give them more zest.

Sorry you have to guess at these amounts, but I don't know how sweet or tart you like your plums. I think I'd use 1 cup water and ½ cup sugar to 4 cups plums. But I don't think I've ever measured. Your guess is as good as mine. They'll have the most gorgeous colour — if you use blue plums — and a tangy taste that is unequalled.

PLUM CRUMBLE

This was the most popular of the six desserts I made for a coffee-dessert party for ladies who are all good cooks.

1 cup flour
1 cup rolled oats
1 cup brown sugar, packed
½ cup melted butter
1 teaspoon cinnamon
4 cups plums, cut in half
1 cup sugar
2 tablespoons cornstarch
1 cup water
1 teaspoon vanilla or almond flavouring

Mix flour, oats, brown sugar, butter, and cinnamon until crumbly. Press half the crumbs into a buttered 9" x 9" baking pan (Pyrex is the best). Cover with plums. Combine remaining ingredients. Cook until thick and clear. Pour over the plums, then top with remaining crumbs. Bake at 350°F for about 45 minutes — it should be golden and rich. Cut into squares and serve.

PLUM FOOL

This a favourite British way of dealing with plums.

Put any number of **whole plums** and a very small amount of **water** into a large saucepan, cover and cook slowly over low heat till the plums are soft. Put them through a sieve, discarding the pits and skin that remain. The result should be a smooth and fairly thick purée. Sweeten to taste — some plums will need more **sugar** than others.

Set the plums aside until they are completely cold, then stir in **fresh thick cream**, in an amount equal to the amount of plums. Refrigerate to chill thoroughly, but do not freeze. The result is smooth, rich, and light. My Devon friend Kath says that actually many British cooks stir in thick cornstarch-custard sauce in place of the cream; it's more economical. You know how the British are always putting custard on their desserts — even an apple pie or gooseberry tart.

SAUCY PLUM DUMPLINGS

This is a really good old Mennonite dessert, and fun to make. You can use canned or stewed plums.

4 cups plums with syrup
1 cup sugar
1 tablespoon cornstarch
1 tablespoon lemon juice or
½ teaspoon cinnamon

Dumplings:
1 cup flour
2 teaspoons baking powder
1 tablespoon sugar
½ teaspoon salt
2 tablespoons melted butter
½ cup milk

Drain the syrup from the plums and pit them. In a broad saucepan, combine sugar, cornstarch, and lemon juice with the plum syrup and heat to boiling, stirring until slightly thickened. Add the plums and bring to a simmer again before you drop in the dumplings.

Sift together the flour, baking powder, sugar, and salt. Blend in the butter. Add milk and stir just enough to moisten. From a spoon, drop the dumpling batter on top of the simmering fruit, cover with a tight-fitting lid and cook gently for 12 to 15 minutes. Don't uncover the pan during the cooking: have faith that the right thing is happening. Serve the dumplings promptly with the plums and plum sauce and plain or whipped cream.

COMPANY DESSERTS

I love luscious desserts and revel in excuses to make them, but I avoid temptation by never making any except when my family and friends come for a meal and on rare occasions when I have a dessert and coffee party or entertain my University Women's Club Book Group. Then I can splurge.

Last time I was planning what I would have, my sister Norm said, "Make only one thing or everyone will want to taste everything and you won't have enough." But how could I enjoy making the same thing five times? One taste and I'd have had it all.

I followed my own inclination and came up with Baba au Rhum, Plum Crumble, Grand Marnier Cafe, Sour Cream Peach Pie, mixed fruit in a bowl, and Jean Salter's Seed Cake.

Norma was right: everyone tried everything. Nothing was left except a feeling of satisfaction that my part had been a success.

BAKED BANANAS

Company coming and nothing in the house for dessert but a few aging bananas? Dress them up this easy way, and your guests will ask for your recipe.

> ½ cup orange juice or
>   2 tablespoons frozen juice
> ½ cup sherry
> ¼ cup brown sugar
> ¼ teaspoon nutmeg
> ¼ teaspoon cinnamon
> 1 tablespoon butter
> 4 bananas
> 2 tablespoons rum

In a saucepan, combine orange juice, sherry, brown sugar, nutmeg, and cinnamon. Add butter and set over low heat. (Don't let it boil.) While it is heating, peel the bananas, split them lengthwise, and place them in a buttered 8" x 8" baking dish. Pour the heated ingredients over the bananas and bake at 400°F for 10 to 15 minutes, or until the bananas are tender, basting once or twice. Take the bananas out of the oven, sprinkle with rum, and serve them hot or warm as you please.

BANANA PRUNE WHIP

This is a tart little dessert to whip up in your blender.

>   10 pitted prunes
>   ½ cup water
>   2 tablespoons lemon juice
>   2 ripe bananas
>   2 or 3 tablespoons dark brown sugar or honey
>   ⅓ cup light cream
>   Chopped pecans

Put the prunes in a saucepan with the water and lemon juice. Simmer for 5 minutes then let cool in the liquid. Pour the whole bit into your blender with the bananas broken into chunks, the sugar, and cream. Spin until the mixture is thick and light. Divide it among 4 serving dishes; it deserves stemmed glasses. Chill for at least an hour, garnish with chipped pecans and watch the happy faces.

LEMON FOAM

A cool, fresh dessert to finish off a heavy meal.

>   Grated rind and juice of 2 large lemons
>   1 cup sugar
>   2 cups water
>   ¼ cup cornstarch
>   2 egg whites
>   Pinch of salt
>   Custard Sauce (page 85)

Place grated rind and juice in a saucepan with sugar and water. Bring slowly to boil, stirring until sugar dissolves. Blend cornstarch to a smooth paste with a little cold water. Add to lemon mixture, stir over heat until thickened. Cool. Whisk egg whites stiffly with salt. Beat cooled lemon mixture until smooth, fold in the stiff egg whites, and pour into a large glass serving bowl. Chill until serving time. Serve with Custard Sauce made with the egg yolks or pour into a baked pie shell and chill.

LEMON SYLLABUB

This is the favourite dessert at Rundles Restaurant in Stratford. The *chef de cuisine* whips it up in a few minutes, the guests linger lovingly over every sip.

¾ cup fine granulated sugar
½ cup dry white wine
Grated rind and juice of 2 large lemons
2 cups whipping cream

Whisk the sugar and white wine. Add both lemon rind and juice to the sugar-wine mixture and blend well. Add the cream and whisk until thick and light. (You can do this with your electric mixer.) Pour into individual wine glasses, chill for 2 hours, garnish with a twist of lemon and a sprig of mint. At Rundles they serve it with a couple of lady fingers and listen to the exclamations of delight.

CARUSO'S CHOCOLATE SOUFFLÉ

When Dottie and I stayed at Amalfi, we went one day to Ravello, high above the sparkling blue Mediterranean. We had a superb lunch at the Hotel Belvedere, and the dessert was its crowning glory. Mr. Caruso — the proprietor, and cousin of the great Enrico — gave us his cherished recipe.

The soufflé came in individual baking dishes, puffed up and enormous, but it melted away into us like snow on a sunny morning. These are the ingredients for one; just increase them to make more.

2 eggs, separated
1 tablespoon sugar
1 tablespoon cocoa
A few spoonfuls of cherry preserves (optional)

Beat the egg whites and yolks separately. Add the yolks to the whites, stirring them in very gently. Blend together the sugar and cocoa, then fold into egg mixture, little by little. Pour into a buttered baking dish in which has been spread a thin layer of cherry preserve. Bake at 350°F until soufflé rises, about 40 to 50 minutes. Serve at once, before it drops.

PAVLOVA

In 1984, my sisters and I went on a bus tour of New Zealand. Our first dinner in that lovely green sheep-covered country was in the city of Christchurch. The meal was a triumph, crowned with Pavlova, the national dish of Down Under. We were told no fruit is as good as passionfruit, but we were in New Zealand in their autumn and passionfruit must have been out of season. We thought nothing could have been better than the fresh strawberries served from a large glass bowl. As we travelled around the country, Pavlova was on the menus of the first-rate motels, but only the first day was it served with fresh strawberries. It was good with canned Australian peaches, or bananas, or tinned pineapple, or mixed fruit. And sometimes there was ice cream instead of whipped cream. Delicious.

Cornstarch
3 egg whites
1 cup sugar
1 teaspoon cornstarch
½ teaspoon white vinegar
½ teaspoon vanilla
Sweetened whipped cream
Fruit

First, draw a 10-inch circle on a piece of brown paper. Grease the paper and put it on a cookie sheet, then sprinkle it lightly with cornstarch. Beat the egg whites until stiff, adding the sugar a teaspoonful at a time, blending in 1 teaspoon cornstarch with the last few spoonfuls. Fold in the vinegar and vanilla. Pour the mixture on the prepared circle, then spread it with a spatula so it is pie-shaped or looks like a cake. Place in bottom of a 200°F oven for 1½ to 2 hours, or until crisp but not browned. Open the oven door and let it cool before removing. Invert it carefully on a cake rack and gently peel off the paper. When cold, slide it on a serving plate. Fill the slightly sunken middle with sweetened whipped cream and cover it with fruit.

NORM'S PERFECT MERINGUES

Norm makes meringues that are always crisp but not hard, never tough or troublesome to eat with a fork or a spoon. One time I had a meringue served to me, and when I attacked it, it jumped right off my plate to the floor. It was not one of Norm's.

6 egg whites, at room temperature
¼ teaspoon salt
1½ teaspoons water
2 teaspoons vinegar or lemon juice
1½ cups white sugar
⅔ teaspoon almond flavoring

Beat the egg whites with the salt, water, and vinegar until soft peaks form. Add the sugar gradually, beating all the while. Continue beating until the meringue is glossy and very firm. You can't overdo it. On greased foil or brown paper on a baking sheet, with a spoon and knife, shape the meringue into 3- to 4-inch rounds, building up the sides to a depth of 1½ inches. They should look like nests. Bake in a 275°F oven for about an hour, or preheat your oven to 375°F, turn it off, put the shells in and let them stay there till the oven cools.

Norm stashes the cold baked shells away in tightly covered tin boxes. When she needs them, she fills them with lemon butter or ice cream with chocolate or butterscotch sauce or with sliced strawberries or peaches alone or over ice cream. Think of all the things you could use to fill the meringue shells. All of them glamorous and delicious.

BABAS AU RHUM

This is a great company dessert; people are really impressed with babas — perhaps because the recipe came from France, but mostly because they are super-elegantly delicious. The babas can be frozen and heated when you need them, and the sauce made days in advance.

¼ cup milk
½ cup butter
1 tablespoon yeast
¼ cup lukewarm water
3 eggs at room temperature
¼ cup sugar
1½ cup flour, sifted
1 tablespoon rum
½ cup chopped citron, mixed peel, or currants
Hot Rum Sauce (see below)

Scald the milk, add the butter, blend and let cool to lukewarm. Sprinkle the yeast on the lukewarm water and stir till dissolved. Beat the eggs, gradually add the sugar then the milk mixture and the yeast. Stir in 1 cup of the flour, the rum and the citron, then the rest of the flour. Beat until smooth.

Cover and let rise in a warm place until doubled, about 1 hour. Stir down and spoon the bubbly batter into greased muffin tins or custard cups and let rise again until doubled. Bake in a 400°F oven for about 10 minutes — test with a cake tester — or bake at 350°F for about 20 minutes. Remove from pans and pour over them the following Rum Sauce. Or cool them, wrap them in foil and freeze them. Reheat and marinate the babas in the hot rum sauce several hours before serving.

HOT RUM SAUCE

1 cup brown sugar
1 cup corn syrup
½ cup water
1 tablespoon butter
½ cup dark rum

Heat all but the rum to boiling point, stirring occasionally. Add the rum. Pour over the warm babas and let them soak up enough sauce to make them moist and spongy. They should be served warm.

For a party, I put my babas in a wide dish that holds them all. Alongside I have a glass bowl filled with whipped cream to blob over each serving. If you prefer, you could serve each baba individually, ignite a couple of ounces of dark rum in a ladle and pour it over the babas. Impressive, as I've said, but I prefer to let my guests help themselves from a large flat dish. There's never a baba left over.

MOCHA TORTE
for John's Birthday Party

John would have no other. Ruby says it will serve twelve generously but has been known to be eaten by eight.

Buy or make a **9½-inch angel cake**. Slice it carefully into 5 horizontal layers.

> **1 cup butter or margarine**
> **1½ cups icing sugar**
> **Pinch of salt**
> **1 teaspoon vanilla**
> **2 eggs, separated**
> **2 squares bitter chocolate, melted**
> **6 tablespoons double-strength coffee**
> **Sweetened whipped cream**
> **Vanilla**

Cream butter and icing sugar, add salt, vanilla, and egg yolks. Beat thoroughly, then add chocolate and coffee. Beat egg whites until stiff and fold in. Spread filling between layers of cake and chill overnight.

In the early afternoon of the party, ice the torte with whipped cream sweetened and flavoured with vanilla. Garnish with curls of semi-sweet chocolate, or whatever you like. Chill until you stick in the candles.

TRIFLE

Sometimes Mother made a Daffodil Sponge Cake, light, high, and pretty to look at, but uninteresting after a day or two; none of us ate much because we so greatly preferred the trifle Mother made with what was left over.

Custard sauce:
2 tablespoons flour
½ cup sugar
Pinch of salt
2 eggs
2 cups milk
1 teaspoon vanilla

Half a sponge cake, lady fingers, or any other dry cake
½ cup red jelly or jam
⅓ cup sherry, brandy, or rum
¼ cup chopped nuts
1 cup whipping cream

To make custard sauce: mix flour, sugar, and salt. Beat the eggs lightly and blend with the sugar mixture. Scald the milk and gradually add it to the other mixture. Cook in a double boiler over hot water, stirring constantly until the sauce thickens and coats a wooden spoon. Cool, add vanilla and chill.

To combine trifle: cut the cake in strips and spread jam generously on the pieces. Criss-cross ¼ of the pieces of cake in a pretty bowl, sprinkle them with a little of the sherry — enough to moisten the cake but not make it soggy. Sprinkle on a few nuts and ¼ of the custard sauce. Repeat this performance till all the cake, jam, sherry, nuts and custard are used up — the custard on top. Chill a few hours; then, before serving, top with whipped cream and chopped nuts.

DEVIL'S FOOD PUDDING WITH ICE-CREAM SAUCE

This is terrific, the sauce is divine; the recipe came from a friend's grandmother.

> 3 squares unsweetened chocolate
> 1½ cups sugar
> 1½ cups milk
> ½ cup shortening
> 2 eggs
> 2 cups flour
> ½ teaspoon salt
> 1 teaspoon vanilla
> 1 teaspoon baking soda mixed with
> 1 tablespoon water
> Ice-Cream Sauce (see below)

Melt the chocolate in a saucepan, add ½ cup of the sugar and ½ cup of the milk. Cook until thick; cool. Blend shortening with remaining sugar and the eggs; stir in the chocolate mixture. Add remaining milk alternately with the flour sifted with salt. Add vanilla, then baking soda, mixed with water. Bake in a tube pan at 325°F for almost an hour — or steam for 40 minutes, then bake at 325°F for 10 minutes. Serve with Ice-Cream Sauce.

ICE-CREAM SAUCE

> ¾ cup sugar
> 1 egg
> ⅛ teaspoon salt
> ⅓ cup melted butter or shortening
> 1 teaspoon vanilla
> 1 cup cream, whipped

Beat together the sugar, egg, and salt. Add the melted butter and beat well. Add the vanilla. Fold in the whipped cream — and that's it, devilishly tempting you to eat far more than you ought to.

EASY ALMOND CHEESECAKE

Don't be deceived by the simplicity of this; it's very rich.

> 24 graham crackers
> ½ cup brown sugar
> ½ cup butter
> 1 4-ounce package cream cheese
> ¼ teaspoon vanilla
> ½ teaspoon almond extract
> 2 eggs
> ½ cup sugar
> Pinch of salt
> 1 cup sour cream

Break graham wafers into crumbs. Mix crumbs with brown sugar and butter, then press into an unbuttered 8" x 8" pan. Cream the cream cheese. Add vanilla and almond extract, then the eggs, sugar, and salt. Beat until smooth, then blend in the sour cream. Pour the mixture over the wafer crust and bake at 375°F for 25 minutes. Chill before serving.

LEMON SOUFFLÉ

This page in Bevvy's notebook is badly spattered over this one.

> 1 cup white sugar
> 2 heaping tablespoons flour
> 1 tablespoon melted butter
> 2 eggs, separated
> Juice and grated rind of 1 lemon
> 1 cup milk

Stir together the sugar and flour, blend in the butter, beaten egg yolks, lemon juice, rind, and milk; lightly fold in the stiffly beaten egg whites. Pour into greased baking dish and set the dish in a pan of water. Cook in 350°F oven for about half an hour — there will be a tender, spongy part on top and a lemony sauce underneath. Perfect after a heavy dinner.

BAKED CUSTARD

So good for the children — and you.

3 eggs
½ teaspoon salt
¼ cup sugar
2 cups milk, scalded
1 teaspoon vanilla
Cinnamon

Beat the eggs, adding the salt and sugar to them; stir in the hot milk slowly, add vanilla and pour into a baking dish. Dust the top with cinnamon and bake at 350°F for almost an hour. Test by putting a silver knife into the middle; if it comes out cleam the custard is done.

MAPLE CUSTARD

Can be made the same way, putting in **⅓ cup maple syrup** and **1⅔ cups milk**.

CHOCOLATE CUSTARD

Add an **ounce of bitter chocolate** to the milk when it is put on to scald and be sure it is all melted before you mix in the eggs. You might want more sugar.

Dream Food

Some of these recipes you should just read and dream about; don't make them often — unless you aren't afraid of gaining weight.

When I bake something, I'm always eager to know how it tastes. I'm not a glutton, I'm just curious. Often one bite would suffice — unless that bite is so delicious that I lose all my resolve.

MOCHA RUM MOUSSE

Lorna says this is a quick and easy one to prepare in your blender.

>   6 ounces semi-sweet chocolate pieces
>   5 tablespoons hot strong coffee
>   4 eggs, separated
>   2 tablespoons light rum

Put the chocolate, coffee, egg yolks, and rum in your blender; cover and blend at high speed for 1 minute. Beat the egg whites until stiff but not dry. Slowly pour in the chocolate mixture, and with a spatula fold until no egg white shows. Spoon into sherbet glasses and refrigerate for 1 hour at least. Top with whipped cream — if you think you must.

CHOCOLATE MINT MOUSSE

My downfall.

>   9 chocolate-covered mint patties
>   1 teaspoon water
>   2 eggs, separated
>   ½ cup whipping cream, plus more for topping

Heat the patties and water in a double boiler, stirring until the patties are melted and the mixture is smooth but not really hot. Beat in the egg yolks one at a time, stir for 1 minute over the heat of the double boiler. Cool. Fold the cooled chocolate mixture into the stiffly beaten egg whites. Then gently fold in the stiffly whipped cream. Spoon into individual stemmed glasses. You don't need much. Chill until serving time. Garnish with green tinted whipped cream and a green cherry or sprig of mint.

POT DE CRÈME CHOCOLAT

This is a lot of bother, but it's worth it. It's very rich: a little goes a long way. I serve mine in demi-tasse with a small coffee spoon on the saucer.

4 eggs, separated
¾ cup sugar
¼ cup Cointreau
6 1-ounce squares semisweet chocolate
¼ cup strong coffee
¾ cup softened butter
Pinch of salt
Whipped cream

Beat the egg yolks and sugar until pale yellow and thick; beat in the liqueur. Place bowl over hot water and keep beating for 10 minutes, or until mixture is foamy. Place bowl over cold water and beat until mixture cools and is the consistency of mayonnaise. In a double boiler, melt the chocolate in the coffee. Remove from heat and beat in the butter a little at a time until smooth. Beat the chocolate mixture into the egg mixture. Beat egg whites with salt until soft peaks form. Stir into chocolate mixture. Spoon into serving dishes and chill for at least 2 hours. Garnish with whipped cream.

GINGER OR CHOCOLATE WAFER DESSERT

For a good reason this recipe has been popular for a long time. Buy a package of **very thin ginger or chocolate wafers**. Whip some **cream**, add **sugar** and **flavouring** then slather whipped cream over the wafers and stack them in neat little piles that will be enough for individual servings. Ice each stack with the whipped cream and serve. I like my wafers crisp but Mother used to let them stand till the cream had softened them slightly.

SYLLABUB

As simple as the length of this recipe makes it look. And divine.

**¾ cup sugar
2 cups Sauterne
3 cups cream
Nutmeg**

Mix sugar, Sauterne, and cream together and beat until frothy. Serve in glasses with a sprinkling of nutmeg.

St. Jean Port Joli

When Marnie and I drove to the east coast to do research for Whatever Happened to Maggie, *we kept as close to the south shore of the St. Lawrence as we could, and we went through all the lovely little French Canadian villages. At St. Jean Port Joli, "the wood-carving capital of Quebec," we had lunch in a large handsome restaurant whose walls were decorated with Quebec scenes carved in wood by Jean Caron, St. Jean's most famous carver.*

We made the mistake of sitting in the room where the Rotary Club was going to be meeting that day, and were asked to go into another dining room. The lunch was acceptable but not memorable — except the dessert we chose. It was a Quebec specialty, and the most expensive item on the dessert menu. When it arrived, we were surprised to find a piece of white bread liberally covered with crumbled maple sugar and soaked in rich sweet cream. It was delicious, and the waitress told us it is a favourite family dessert in La Belle Province.

CREAM PUFFS

Here is Mother's recipe.

> ½ cup butter
> 1 cup boiling water
> 1 cup sifted flour
> 4 eggs
> Sweetened whipped cream

Put butter and water into a saucepan and boil until the butter is melted. Stirring rapidly, add flour and cook until mixture is thick and smooth. Scrape into a mixing bowl and when lukewarm add one egg at a time, beating after each addition until the mixture is very smooth. Drop by spoonfuls on a greased baking sheet at least 1½ inches apart. Bake in a 400°F oven about 35 minutes. When cool, make a slit in the side of each great puffy thing with a pair of scissors and fill with sweetened whipped cream.

CHOCOLATE DESSERT

This is a smoothie that will quickly win warm approval.

> 3 heaping tablespoons flour
> 1 heaping tablespoon cocoa
> ½ teaspoon salt
> 1 cup sugar
> 2 cups boiling water
> Butter the size of an egg
> 1 teaspoon vanilla
> Whipped cream

Blend the flour, cocoa, salt, and sugar in a little cold water. Add the boiling water and cook until thick — it takes a little over 10 minutes. After it is taken from the stove, add the butter and vanilla. Stir until smooth. Pour into a serving dish and chill. Serve with a mound of whipped cream on top and perhaps a few nuts, but don't keep on tasting (and diminishing) it before it reaches the table!

RICE AND TAPIOCA PUDDINGS

Have you noticed how often men order rice pudding instead of more sophisticated treats from a restaurant menu? Is it because their wives don't make them at home as their mothers did and the men are nostalgic?

My mother's rice and tapioca puddings were among our favourite desserts.

CREAMY RICE PUDDING

When I was eight years old, I visited my father's Aunt Nellie for three weeks and I'm sure we had rice pudding for dessert every meal — dry, boiled, flavourless rice, with milk and sugar sprinkled over it. I wished Auntie Nellie could cook rice nice and creamy like Mother's. This way:

> ½ cup uncooked rice
> ¼ teaspoon salt
> 2 cups whole milk
> ½ cup raisins
> 2 eggs, separated
> ½ cup sugar
> 1 teaspoon vanilla
> Cinnamon

Put the rice, salt, and milk in a double boiler and cook until the rice is tender — about ¾ of an hour. If it seems dry, add more milk. At half-time put in the raisins. Beat the egg yolks, add the sugar, stir some of the hot rice into the mixture, then add to the rice in the double boiler and cook for 2 or 3 minutes, stirring all the time. Remove from heat, stir in vanilla and a generous sprinkling of cinnamon. Add more milk (or cream), if it is dry; it should be moist.

Let it cool a bit. It should not be quite cold when you serve it topped by a perky mound of the **egg whites beaten stiff**, with **4 teaspoons sugar** and a couple of drops of **vanilla**.

LORNA'S CHOCOLATE RICE PUDDING

The cooking smells were tantalizing one day while my family and I were playing Parcheesi. We could hardly wait to eat.

2 cups cooked rice
2 cups milk
½ cup sugar
3 tablespoons cocoa
½ teaspoon salt
1 teaspoon vanilla
Piece of butter (the size depends on your waistline)

Put the cooked rice and milk in the top of a double boiler, mix the sugar, cocoa, and salt and stir into the rice. Cook over gently boiling water for 45 minutes. Keep looking at it and give it a stir now and then. It should be creamy, not stiff. Add the vanilla and butter before serving.

Don't Diet

Never go on a diet. They say it does you no good: sudden weight loss results in sudden weight gain immediately after. Never do anything drastic or silly, like living on cottage cheese, or drinking beer and eating no food, or any of those fancy fad diets you read about. Simply eat less of everything you need to keep healthy — and no luscious desserts every day, or fatty things, or fried ones. If you feel hungry, get out a cookbook and read some rich, gloopy recipes that you know you would never dare make or eat. Read them slowly, comfortably imagining yourself eating them. Then go to sleep or have a glass of water or milk, or go for a walk, or phone a friend. Don't, don't, don't go out to the kitchen and nibble on peanuts or cookies or a piece of pie. If you must stop the gnawing, eat a carrot or a stick of celery. But I don't have to tell you that — you've heard it before, and like me, you haven't done it. You've gone for the peanuts or chocolates, or those last few cookies left in the jar.

Maple Rice Pudding

A variation of Lorna's Chocolate Rice Pudding. Instead of sugar, cocoa, and vanilla use **½ cup maple syrup** and only **1½ cups milk**.

TAPIOCA PUDDING

Fish eyes and glue we used to call the half-cooked, large-grained, starchy tapioca without flavour that we were served every week in our residence at university. How I longed for the creamy pudding Mother used to make.

    3 cups milk
    ¼ cup quick tapioca or big tapioca soaked in water overnight
    ½ cup sugar
    ½ teaspoon salt
    1 egg, separated
    1 teaspoon vanilla

Scald the milk in a double boiler and add tapioca, sugar, and salt. Cook until the tapioca is clear, stirring often. Pour some of the tapioca mixture over beaten egg yolk, stirring rapidly; return to double boiler and cook until mixture thickens. Remove from fire, add vanilla and fold in the stiffly beaten egg white — or make a meringue of the egg white to serve with the tapioca after it has been chilled.

Chocolate Tapioca Pudding

Add **1½ squares melted unsweetened chocolate** or blend **⅓ cup cocoa** with the sugar before adding to hot milk in the recipe above.

BAKED PUDDINGS

I get thousands of letters from fans, and most of them tell me they like my books because they can read the recipes and go right into their kitchens and make them with whatever they have in their cupboard or fridge. These baked puddings should add to your list of desserts to be made on a blustery day when you want some adventure in the house.

SNOW ON THE MOUNTAIN

Ever invite people for dinner at very short notice — like maybe two hours? This is an easy dessert that always pleases the chocolate lovers. It should be enough for six.

> ½ cup milk (you can use milk powder and water)
> 2 1-ounce squares unsweetened chocolate, coarsely ground, or ½ cup cocoa
> 3 tablespoons butter
> ½ cup sugar
> 1 egg
> ½ teaspoon vanilla
> ½ cup flour
> ½ teaspoon salt
> 1 teaspoon baking powder
> Mallow Mint Sauce (page 88)

Heat the milk in a double boiler over hot water or in a heavy pan at medium heat. Add chocolate. Cook until thick, stirring to keep it smooth. Blend butter, sugar, and egg until light. Add chocolate mixture and vanilla. Sift flour, salt, and baking powder into chocolate mixture. Pour into 6 buttered custard cups and bake at 350°F for almost 20 minutes. Unmould and serve warm with Mallow Mint Sauce.

DESSERTS

HOT FUDGE PUDDING

This is a dandy little pudding to make on a winter day. Ruby says she always made this when her family was mad at her. Then they weren't.

    1 cup sifted flour
    ¾ cup sugar
    2 teaspoons baking powder
    ½ teaspoon salt
    6 tablespoons cocoa
    ½ cup milk
    1 teaspoon vanilla
    3 tablespoons melted shortening
    ¾ cup chopped walnuts
    ¾ cup brown sugar
    2 tablespoons butter, melted
    1¾ cups hot water

Sift the dry ingredients and 2 tablespoons of the cocoa. Stir together the milk, vanilla, and melted shortening; add to the dry ingredients, mix well, then stir in the nuts. Pour into a 9" x 9" pan. Now mix the brown sugar and 4 remaining tablespoons cocoa; sprinkle the mixture over the batter in the pan. Pour on the melted butter then carefully pour on the hot water. Bake at 350°F for about 40 minutes. Serve hot. They'll love you for this.

BEVVY'S SEVEN-CENT PUDDING

Those were the days!

    1½ cups flour
    1 cup sugar
    1 teaspoon baking soda
    ½ teaspoon baking powder
    1½ cups oatmeal
    ½ cup cream
    ½ cup buttermilk

Sift dry ingredients, add oatmeal; add cream and buttermilk. Pour into a 9" x 9" pan and bake in 350°F oven for about 30 minutes. Serve with crushed fruit as a sauce.

QUICK PUDDING

This was baking in Bevvy's oven while we were eating our supper; I wished I'd saved more room for it.

⅓ cup sugar
½ cup milk
1 cup raisins
1 cup flour
1 teaspoon baking powder

Mix in the order given and put into greased baking dish. Over it pour: **½ cup brown sugar**, dissolved in **1 cup boiling water,** and a piece of **butter the size of an egg**. Bake 30 minutes at 350°F. The dough part comes to the top and is surrounded by rich brown sauce.

TWENTY-MINUTE DESSERT

Worth trying. It's really good — dumplings in caramel sauce.

1½ cups brown sugar
2 cups boiling water
2 tablespoons butter

Stir all together in a cooking pot till sugar has dissolved; add butter and simmer while you mix the dumplings:

1 tablespoon butter
½ cup sugar
½ teaspoon salt
1½ cups flour
1 tablespoon baking powder
½ cup milk

Cream butter, sugar, and salt, add sifted flour and baking powder alternately with milk to make a stiff batter. Drop by tablespoonfuls into boiling sauce — or maple syrup — cover and let boil gently for about 15 minutes. Serve warm.

COTTAGE PUDDING

Quick and good.

1 cup brown sugar
3 tablespoons melted butter
½ teaspoon salt
2 eggs, beaten
1 cup buttermilk
2 cups flour
2 teaspoons cream of tartar
1 teaspoon baking soda

Blend the sugar, butter, and salt; beat in the eggs, then add the milk alternately with the dry ingredients sifted together. Bake at 350°F for about half an hour. Serve with any sauce you like.

BREAD PUDDING

Mother told me a thousand times that bread pudding was delicious, healthful, economical, and I *must* eat it.

2 eggs
½ cup sugar, white or brown
2 cups milk
½ teaspoon cinnamon
¼ teaspoon nutmeg
4 cups stale bread cubes (or even stale cake)
¼ cup raisins

Beat the eggs, add the sugar, milk, and spices. Butter a baking dish, arrange bread or cake and raisins in the dish and pour the liquid over it. Let stand until bread has been thoroughly soaked. Bake in a 350°F oven for 25 minutes.

    Knowing how much I liked chocolate, Mother sometimes put in 2 tablespoons of cocoa instead of the spices and served the pudding with a chocolate sauce instead of the usual custard sauce. I was never fooled: it still was bread pudding.

HUNTER'S PUDDING

A woman Norm met in Florida gave her this recipe. I've never liked bread pudding, but I do like this with vanilla ice cream.

¾ cup butter
1½ cups sugar
2 eggs, beaten
1¾ cups milk
1 teaspoon baking powder
¾ teaspoon nutmeg
¾ teaspoon cloves
½ tablespoon cinnamon
6 slices bread, cut into cubes
¾ cup chopped nuts
1½ cups raisins

Cream the butter and sugar. Add the eggs, milk, baking powder, and spices, and blend well. Stir in the bread, nuts, and raisins. Pour into a pan and bake at 350°F for about 1 hour, or until firm. Serve hot.

MAPLE PUDDING

This is a dandy little pudding to make in a hurry. Heat **1 cup maple syrup** to boiling and pour it into a buttered baking dish. Combine the following in the order given:

1 tablespoon lard
3 tablespoons white sugar
2 teaspoons salt
1 egg
½ cup milk
1 cup flour
2 teaspoons baking powder

Pour the batter into the hot maple syrup and bake in a 350°F oven for about 30 minutes. Serve hot or cold.

NEW ORLEANS BREAD PUDDING

Norm and Ralph ordered bread pudding at a restaurant in New Orleans; they liked it so well that they went back next day to have it again and get the recipe from the chef.

> 1½ cups milk
> ¼ cup butter
> 2 cups bread cubes
> 1 cup sugar
> 3 eggs, beaten
> 1 cup raisins
> Sprinkle of cinnamon
> 1 teaspoon rum flavouring,
>   or more of the real thing

Warm the milk, add the butter, and when it has melted, pour the hot liquid over the bread cubes. Soak for about 5 minutes, then add the sugar, eggs, raisins, cinnamon, and rum. Pour the mixture into a buttered 8" x 8" baking dish, set it in a pan of hot water in a 300°F oven and bake about 40 to 50 minutes until the pudding is puffed up and brown and a knife inserted in the centre comes out clean.

Serve with this super sauce:

> 1½ cups sugar
> 2 cups water
> 4 thin slices orange
> 4 thin slices lemon
> ½ to 1 cup rum

Simmer the sugar, water, and fruit slices. Cool and add the rum. Pour a little over the pudding and garnish it with whipped cream.

GELATINE DESSERTS

Gelatine desserts must be made in advance — which is an advantage because they're no problem at the last minute. They are easy to prepare and welcome after a hearty meal. For family or friends.

CITRUS SOUFFLÉ

A tangy light dessert for a meal that makes you feel stuffed.

4 eggs, separated
¾ cup sugar
1 tablespoon grated lemon rind
1 tablespoon grated orange rind
¼ cup lemon juice
½ cup orange juice
1 tablespoon gelatine
1 cup ice-cold evaporated milk
Finely chopped nuts

Beat the egg yolks. Gradually add the sugar and keep beating until thick and creamy. Add lemon and orange rind; add the lemon juice and ¼ cup of the orange juice, then beat another 5 minutes. Over hot water, dissolve gelatine in remaining ¼ cup orange juice. Cool to lukewarm, then stir into egg mixture. Chill until partially set, about 30 minutes. In a large bowl, whip the ice-cold evaporated milk till stiff, then beat in gelatine mixture. Fold in stiffly beaten egg whites. Pour into a pretty serving bowl and chill until set, about 1 hour. Decorate with nuts.

LEMON SNOW

Wonderfully tart and light after a heavy dinner.

>   1 tablespoon gelatine
>   ¼ cup cold water
>   1 cup hot water
>   ¾ cup sugar
>   ¼ teaspoon salt
>   ¼ cup lemon juice
>   Grated rind of 1 lemon
>   2 egg whites, beaten stiff
>   Custard Sauce (page 85)

Dissolve the gelatine in cold water, add hot water, sugar, and salt and stir until dissolved. Add lemon juice and rind. Cool and, when quite thick, beat until frothy. Beat egg whites until stiff, fold into lemon mixture and keep on beating mixture until stiff enough to hold its shape. Put into a pretty serving dish and chill. Serve with custard sauce.

MAPLE MOUSSE

Mother made this often — so smoooooth, and rich and delicate; we loved it.

>   2 teaspoons plain gelatine
>   ¼ cup cold water
>   2 eggs, beaten
>   1 cup maple syrup
>   1 cup cream, whipped

Soak the gelatine in the cold water. Set aside. Beat the eggs and add the maple syrup, cooking the mixture in a double boiler for about 2 minutes, stirring constantly. While the mixture is still hot, add the gelatine and stir in well. Let cool till it is almost thick, then fold in the stiffly whipped cream. Put the mousse in an ice tray in the refrigerator to chill thoroughly. Mother said, "It's good to give it a stir with a fork before it sets."

JELL-O FRUIT PUDDING

Always appreciated.

>   1 package Jell-o powder — any flavour or colour that goes with your decor
>   2 cups boiling water
>   ¼ teaspoon salt
>   ½ cup raisins, chopped
>   12 dates, pitted and chopped
>   1 banana, sliced
>   ¼ cup chopped nuts,
>   **Whipped cream or Ice-Cream Sauce (page 45)**

Dissolve the Jell-o in boiling water, add salt, then chill. When slightly thickened, fold in the fruits and nuts. Turn into a mould and chill until firm. Unmould, serve with whipped cream or Ice-Cream Sauce.

SHERRY SOUFFLÉ

This make-ahead dessert looks special served in stemmed glasses with crisp cookies on the side of the plate.

>   1 tablespoon gelatine
>   ⅓ cup water
>   3 eggs, separated
>   ½ cup sugar
>   ½ cup sherry

Sprinkle the gelatine over the water and allow to soften for a few minutes. Set the bowl over hot water to dissolve. In the top of double boiler, beat the egg yolks, add ¼ cup of the sugar and beat until thick and pale in colour. Add the gelatine and beat well. Gradually beat in the sherry. Set the mixture over simmering water and continue to beat, until it foams and begins to thicken. Be careful not to overcook. Cool, then chill until it begins to set. Beat the egg whites until stiff, then gradually beat in remaining ¼ cup sugar. Fold the egg whites into the chilled egg-yolk mixture. Spoon into tall glasses and chill until ready to hear your guests' exclamations.

RUBY'S LEMON DELIGHT

Ruby says this is the handiest dessert when you need quite a lot. It keeps well, can be made in advance, and really tastes good.

> 2 cups graham wafer crumbs
> ½ cup brown sugar
> ½ cup butter or margarine
> 1 package lemon Jell-o powder
> ½ cup boiling water
> 1 large can evaporated milk
>   (must be icy cold to whip)
> ½ cup sugar
> Juice and grated rind of 1 lemon

Mix graham wafer crumbs with brown sugar and butter. Pack two-thirds of the mixture in the bottom of an unbuttered 9" x 13" pan. Dissolve Jell-o in boiling water and set aside to cool. Whip chilled evaporated milk until stiff. Add sugar and lemon juice and rind, then beat in the Jell-o. Pour the mixture over the crumbs in the pan. Sprinkle remaining crumbs over top and chill in refrigerator for 3 hours, or in freezer for 1 hour. Cut into squares to serve.

GRAND MARNIER CAFÉ

A few tablespoons of brandy, wine, or liqueur can give a bland, easy-to-make dessert both flavour and flair. Watch the reaction of your guests when you tell them your secret ingredient.

> 1 envelope unflavoured gelatine
> 2 cups milk or cream
> 1 rounded tablespoon instant coffee powder
> ½ teaspoon salt
> ¼ cup sugar
> 1 or 2 tablespoons Grand Marnier, or whatever
> 2 egg whites, beaten stiff

Soften the gelatine in the cold milk in a saucepan, add the coffee powder and heat, stirring until the gelatine and coffee are dissolved, no longer. Add salt and sugar, then chill until it is slightly thickened. Stir in the Grand Marnier, Cointreau, or whatever you prefer or have. Fold in the stiffly beaten egg whites. Pour the lovely stuff into a glass bowl that will show it off, or into individual frosted sherbets. Let it set — a day ahead of your party if you like. A piece of fruit cake goes well with it.

QUIVERING EGGNOG

Easy and soothing at Christmas time.

> 2 cups milk
> 1 cup cream
> ½ cup rum or sherry
> ½ cup sugar
> 3 eggs
> 1 teaspoon vanilla
> **Dash of salt**
> **Sprinkle of nutmeg**

Put all this in your blender and give it a good whirl — then don't drink it. Give it a chance to quiver.

> **2 envelopes gelatine moistened in ¼ cup water**
> **¾ cup hot milk**

Dissolve the moistened gelatine in the hot milk, pour it into the blender with the eggnog, whirl for a second then pour it into a pretty glass bowl and keep it in a cool place till it is set. Sprinkle nutmeg on top and serve it with Christmas cake and cookies.

COFFEE JELLY

You wouldn't waste leftover coffee, would you? All you need is **1 tablespoon gelatine for every 2 cups coffee**.

Moisten the gelatine in ¼ cup cold coffee. Heat ½ cup coffee to almost boiling and stir it into the gelatine till it is dissolved. Add the remaining 1¼ cups cold coffee, stir it well and chill till the jelly sets. Serve it with plain or sweetened **whipped cream** and pass some crisp fresh cookies.

BANANA SPONGE

This won't keep long. For two reasons.

>   **2 tablespoons gelatine**
>   **½ cup cold water**
>   **1 cup sugar**
>   **⅔ cup boiling water**
>   **4 tablespoons lemon juice**
>   **1½ cups mashed bananas**
>   **4 egg whites, stiffly beaten**
>   **Whipped cream or Custard Sauce (page 85)**

Soften gelatine in cold water. Dissolve sugar in boiling water; boil a minute. Remove from heat, add gelatine and dissolve. Add lemon juice and bananas. When partly set, beat; then add stiffly beaten eggs. Chill. Serve with whipped cream or Custard Sauce made with egg yolks.

NEW ORLEANS PRUNE WHIP

I wish I could remember the name of the restaurant in New Orleans that served this. I only know it wasn't Antoine's.

>   **1 tablespoon gelatine**
>   **¼ cup cold water**
>   **½ cup strong coffee**
>   **¼ cup sherry**
>   **Pinch of salt**
>   **½ cup sugar**

¼ cup chocolate chips
1 cup cooked chopped prunes
¼ cup coarsely chopped walnuts
1 cup cream, whipped
Extra cream and nuts

In a double boiler, soak the gelatine in the cold water for 5 minutes. Add the coffee, sherry, salt, sugar, and chocolate; stir until the chocolate is dissolved. Cool. When mixture begins to thicken, stir in the prunes and walnuts, then carefully fold in the whipped cream. Spoon into glasses and top with whipped cream and nuts. Chill before serving.

STRAWBERRY SNOW

This is a refreshing little dessert to serve on a sunny spring day.

1 tablespoon gelatine
¼ cup water
2 cups crushed strawberries
4 egg whites
⅔ cup sugar
1 cup whipping cream
Whole strawberries

Sprinkle the gelatine over the water and allow to soften for 5 minutes. Heat 1 cup crushed strawberries to boiling point, add gelatine, and stir until dissolved. Chill until it begins to thicken. Beat the egg whites until soft peaks form, then gradually beat in the sugar. Fold into the chilled strawberry mixture, then add the remaining cup of crushed strawberries. Whip the cream until stiff and fold it into strawberries. Serve immediately in individual glass dishes, decorated with whole berries.

If you prefer, you may pour this mixture into freezer trays and freeze. It's great to have in reserve.

FROZEN DESSERTS

Keeping a few desserts in your freezer will give you peace of mind. Serve them in stemmed glasses with cookies or cake on the side, or pour a couple of tablespoons of liqueur over them — or maple syrup or a sauce. You'll be giving your guests what is usually the most expensive dessert on a restaurant menu.

Because every morning and evening Eva and Hannah milk twenty or more cows, they are constantly thinking up ways to use a surplus of cream. Always they have plastic containers of ice cream in their freezers, which they serve with chiffon cakes that are seven or eight inches high and covered with icing that takes a half pound of butter.

MARSHMALLOW-COCOA ICE CREAM

We always thought Mother's ice cream was smoother, and more chocolatey than the boughten kind — and more easily available for the little stolen tastes!

12 marshmallows
2 tablespoons sugar
2 tablespoons cocoa
Pinch of salt
½ cup milk
1 cup cream, whipped

In a double boiler, stir till dissolved: the marshmallows, sugar, cocoa, salt, and milk. Cool — but before it sets, add whipped cream. Put the mixture in the fridge, in an ice tray, stirring with a fork before it gets hard.

VANILLA ICE CREAM

This is the easiest way I know to make ice cream. Just keep adding, then beating, then freezing.

> 2 cups whipping cream
> ½ cup sugar
> ½ cup milk
> 1 teaspoon vanilla
> Pinch of salt
> 1 egg

Beat the cream until thick, then add the rest of the ingredients in the order given. Freeze until hard. If you like, you could use another flavouring: peppermint, rum, maple, etc.

EASY ICE CREAM

You can vary the flavour of this ice cream — use your imagination.

> 2 eggs, separated
> ½ cup sugar
> ½ cup whipping cream
> 3 tablespoons orange juice

Beat egg whites until stiff. Gradually add the sugar and beat until it is dissolved. Add egg yolks and beat until thoroughly mixed. Whip cream until thick but not stiff, then fold into egg mixture with fruit juice or flavouring of your choice. Put into a freezer tray and freeze until set. Serve as is, or with rum or caramel sauce.

GINGER ICE CREAM

⅓ cup finely chopped preserved ginger
⅓ cup sugar
⅓ cup water
3 egg yolks, beaten
½ teaspoon gelatine
1 tablespoon cold water
2 cups whipping cream

Cook the ginger, sugar, and water to 230°F then a bit at a time blend it with the beaten egg yolks and cook in a double boiler until it thickens. Soak the gelatine for 5 minutes in the spoonful of water and add it to the ginger mixture while it is hot. Cool it and when it is really cold, but not stiff, fold it into the stiffly whipped cream. Pour into a refrigerator tray and freeze without stirring further. Good.

COFFEE CARAMEL ICE CREAM

Another of Lorna's: for a hot day in July after a long, long swim.

1 cup sugar
1½ cups milk, scalded
3 egg yolks
3 tablespoons flour or 2 tablespoons cornstarch
¼ cup strong coffee
Pinch of salt
2 cups whipping cream
1 teaspoon vanilla

Melt the sugar over low heat until caramel colour; add the scalded milk, stirring continuously. Beat the egg yolks, add the flour, coffee, and salt. Stir into the hot milk and cook on low heat until thickened. Cool in fridge. Whip the cream, add vanilla and the chilled mixture; mix well but not overly. Freeze 2 hours before devouring. Needs no stirring during the process, thus avoiding temptation.

CRANBERRY ICE CREAM

Lorna's recipes are always different, delicious, and lovely to look at.

>2 teaspoons gelatine
>¼ cup cold water
>2 cups cranberry sauce
>½ cup orange juice
>A few grains of salt
>1 tablespoon lemon juice
>2 tablespoons corn syrup
>1¼ cups whipping cream
>1 cup cut-up marshmallows

Soften the gelatine in the cold water. Put cranberry sauce into a pan and mush it until the berries are well broken. Add the orange juice and bring to the scalding point. Stir in the softened gelatine. Add salt, lemon juice, corn syrup. Cool completely. Beat the whipping cream until stiff. Fold in the marshmallows and the cold cranberry mixture. Freeze until firm, stirring once or twice.

MINT PARFAIT

Another easy way to make ice cream. You can vary the flavours, too. Try preserved ginger instead of the peppermint.

>16 marshmallows
>¾ cup milk
>1 3-ounce bottle crème de menthe cherries
>5 drops essence of peppermint
>1 cup whipping cream

Over very low heat or in the top of a double boiler, melt the marshmallows in the milk; keep stirring until the mixture is smooth. Chop the cherries very fine, then add to marshmallows. Stir in juice from the cherries, then add peppermint essence. Let cool. Meanwhile, in a large bowl, beat the cream until stiff peaks form. When mixture is slightly stiffened, carefully combine with stiffly beaten cream. Pour into ice-cube trays and freeze without stirring. Serve in sherbet or parfait glasses.

STRAWBERRY DELIGHT

Light, refreshing and delicious, this was my favourite of the seven desserts Laurie Bennet served at a dessert party on St. Patrick's Day. She made it five days in advance.

Bottom:
½ **cup butter**
¼ **cup brown sugar**
1 **cup flour**
½ **cup chopped pecans**

Top:
2 **cups frozen strawberries**
⅔ **cup white sugar**
2 **egg whites**
1 **cup cold evaporated milk**
1 **tablespoon lemon juice**

Blend the butter, sugar, and flour, add the chopped pecans; pat into an 8" x 13" pan and bake at 350°F for 10 minutes. Then cool. Beat the frozen strawberries, add the sugar. Beat the egg whites till stiff and fold them into the strawberry and sugar mixture. Beat the cold evaporated milk and lemon juice, then add to the strawberry mixture. Pour over the cold crust and freeze till you're ready to use it — if you can avoid its discovery that long.

BANANA ICE

This is an easy dessert to keep on hand in your freezer. It's refreshing and slightly tart. Great with cookies or fruit cake. The recipe came from Mary Akehurst in Tucson, Arizona.

Juice of 1 orange
Juice of 1 lemon
A little finely grated rind of both orange and lemon
2 bananas
⅔ cup sugar
1 cup milk
Whipped cream

Place all ingredients except whipped cream in the blender and blend for 1 minute. Pour into an ice-cube tray and freeze. To serve, let it stand at room temperature for a few minutes. Cut into squares and serve with whipped cream over it.

LEMON-WATER ICE

This is perfect with spicy cookies or gingerbread — or just so.

¾ cup sugar
2 cups water
½ cup lemon juice
1 teaspoon grated lemon rind
1 egg white
1 tablespoon icing sugar

Put the sugar into a saucepan with the water; stir over low heat until the sugar is dissolved. Stir in the lemon juice and rind, then let cool. Pour into a freezer tray and freeze, stirring occasionally, until mushy. Beat the egg white until stiff. Gradually beat in the icing sugar. Scrape the frozen lemon mixture into a bowl, fold in the egg white, return to the freezer, and serve when you are ready.

PEACH SHERBET

On a hot summer day, what could be more welcome than sherbet?

    ⅔ cup sweetened condensed milk
    1 tablespoon lemon juice
    1 tablespoon melted butter
    ½ cup water
    1 cup mashed peaches
    Peach brandy
    2 egg whites

Combine the sweetened condensed milk, lemon juice, butter, and water. Sprinkle the peaches lightly with brandy, then stir into milk mixture. Chill. Beat egg whites until stiff, then fold them into chilled mixture. Pour into a freezer tray and place in the freezer. When half frozen, empty into a chilled bowl and beat until smooth but not melted. Return to freezer tray and freeze until firm. Serve in sherbet glasses.

MOCHA NUT TORTONI

Lorna gave us this super dessert one night at dinner; she served it in the little glass dishes in which it was frozen, eliminating the temptation to have second helpings — which we certainly didn't need, but longed to have.

    2 eggs, separated
    ½ cup sugar
    2 cups whipping cream
    2 tablespoons instant coffee powder
    1 teaspoon vanilla
    ½ cup semi-sweet chocolate pieces, or 2 squares
    ½ cup minced, toasted almonds

Beat the egg whites until quite stiff; then gradually add ¼ cup of the sugar while beating. Whip the cream with other ¼ cup sugar and coffee. Add the beaten egg yolks and vanilla. Fold into the stiffly beaten egg whites. Melt the chocolate over hot, but not boiling, water, then cool slightly; quickly fold the chocolate and almonds into the egg-white mixture. Turn into 12 custard cups or 16 two-ounce paper soufflé cups. Freeze until firm then freezer-wrap and freeze longer. To serve garnish with almonds and whipped cream. It was so gooooood.

BANANA SPLIT

There was always action in Clara May's kitchen, and I loved to sit there and listen whenever I visited Neil's Harbour.

"You finish the sweepin', Maggie, I'm so tired tonoight I'm roight shaky," Clara May flopped on a chair near me. "Got Henry and the boys up fer fishin' and swordfishin' this morning and ain't sat down since." She fanned her flushed face with her hand. "Went on a little trip yesterday and had twice as much work today".

"Where was you to? I looked over here and didn't see you around," The older woman who spoke was a neighbour.

"Oh, dear Lord, Maude, wait till I tells you," Clara May's vigour came back. "Mr. Carey come over from Ingonish and took Lily and me to Dingwall. We had the grandest droive, went roight down to the sand, then we stopped at a restaurant at Cape North — just as noice as any you'd see in town — and he bought us a banana split." She paused ecstatically, "Moi dear, I does love a banana split!"

In northern Cape Breton, bananas weren't seen very often. A banana split was the ultimate treat.

Cut a **banana** lengthwise and put both pieces in a dish long enough to accommodate them. Put several scoops of **ice cream** on top and then pour over them and the bananas whatever you like: **strawberry or raspberry jam** makes it look nice, but you might prefer **butterscotch or chocolate sauce** with **nuts** sprinkled over top. A banana split is anyone's creation.

PATSY BEAN'S QUICK, EASY AND DELICIOUS DESSERT

Patsy says this is the best dessert she knows. You can make it in 5 minutes, keep it indefinitely, serve it any time, and everyone loves it.

> 5 cups Rice Crispies
> 1 cup melted butter
> 1 cup coconut
> ½ cup white or brown sugar, or half of each
> Ice cream

"Slosh it all except the ice cream together till it's well mixed," Patsy says. "Use your hands, it's messy but easier." Put half of it into a buttered Pyrex cake pan — a big one. Cover it with ice cream, as thick as you like, then put the other half of the mixture on top. Put it in your freezer where it will turn hard and keep as long as you let it. You need a sharp knife to cut it, that's all. Patsy says you can double or triple it if you need it for a crowd.

STRAWBERRIES QUÉBÉCOIS

You pay a lot for this in the dining rooms of the luxury hotels in Quebec City.

> 1 cup whipping cream
> 2 cups vanilla ice cream
> 4 cups strawberries
> 1 tablespoon sugar
> 1 liqueur glass Cointreau

Whip the cream until stiff. Soften the ice cream slightly, and fold it into the cream. Put into freezer trays and freeze until firm. Wash and hull the strawberries. Sprinkle with sugar. Reserve a few berries for garnish. Before serving, add Cointreau to the strawberries. Let ice cream mixture soften for a few minutes, then fold in the berries. Decorate with a few berries and serve at once.

STEAMED PUDDINGS

If you have an old-fashioned cookstove, you're lucky; you can have a steamed pudding perking away for hours. But even if you haven't, what's wrong with turning on a burner of your electric or gas stove and letting a steamed pudding have its way as it gently humidifies your house. The resulting pudding, moist and tender, can be enjoyed long before you taste it. And when you taste it, you will enjoy it even more.

PREPARING A STEAMED PUDDING

To prepare a steamed pudding: put batter into a greased bowl or mould, two-thirds full; cover it firmly with foil or a lid, then place it on a rack or trivet over one or two inches of water in a large pot or kettle with a tight lid. Start at high heat then let water boil gently for the rest of the cooking time. Take lid from mould and let pudding rest a few minutes before unmoulding.

CHRISTMAS PLUM PUDDING

Too bad Christmas comes only once a year.

> 4 cups flour
> 2 tablespoons baking powder
> 1 teaspoon salt
> 1 teaspoon nutmeg
> 1 teaspoon ginger
> 1 teaspoon cloves
> 1 teaspoon cinnamon
> 1 pound beef suet, chopped fine
> 1½ cups pitted dates
> 5½ cups raisins
> 5 cups currants
> 2½ cups mixed peel, cut-up
> 2 medium-sized apples, cut-up
> 2 carrots, grated
> 2½ cups almonds, chopped
> 4 cups breadcrumbs
> 2 cups milk
> 2½ cups brown sugar
> 4 eggs
> 1 cup molasses
> Brandy Sauce (page 87)

Sift flour, baking powder, salt, and spices together. Chop the suet finely and add chopped dates, raisins, currants and cut-up peel, apples, carrots, and almonds; mix thoroughly and combine with flour mixture. Soak the breadcrumbs in the milk, add sugar, well-beaten eggs, and molasses; combine with first mixture. Turn into well-greased moulds, cover and steam (see page 78) for six hours. Serve with Brandy Sauce.

ENGLISH CHRISTMAS PUDDING

An old favourite of Jean Salter's family. Jean's father (now retired) was a pilot who brought the big ships into port at Southampton.

2 cups raisins
1 cup currants
½ cup chopped candied peel
½ cup blanched almonds
1 cup flour
¼ teaspoon salt
1 teaspoon baking powder
1 teaspoon mixed spice
1 teaspoon nutmeg
½ pound beef suet, finely shredded
2 cups dry white breadcrumbs
Grated rind of 1 lemon
6 eggs, beaten
1½ cups brown sugar
¼ cup brandy or rum
Stout or heavy ale to mix

Clean the fruit and chop the peel and almonds. Sift the flour, salt, baking powder, and spices together; add the finely shredded suet and rub it into the flour. Add the fruit, nuts, breadcrumbs, and grated rind. Beat the eggs, brown sugar, and rum together then mix well with the fruit mixture, adding enough stout or ale to give the batter a stiff dropping consistency. It is best if you can leave it to stand overnight before putting into greased bowls. Cover and steam (see page 78) for several hours. Jean says she doubles this recipe because the puddings keep so well from one Christmas to the next, even out of the freezer.

CARROT PUDDING

While I'm eating this, I usually think I like it better than real plum pudding.

>   2 cups cooked and mashed carrots
>   1 cup finely chopped suet
>   1 cup molasses
>   ½ cup raisins
>   ½ cup currants
>   ½ cup citron peel, cut fine
>   ½ cup flour — or enough to stiffen batter
>   1 egg
>   Grated rind of ½ lemon
>   2 tablespoons brown sugar
>   1 teaspoon cinnamon
>   1 teaspoon cloves
>   1 teaspoon nutmeg
>   ½ teaspoon salt
>   1 teaspoon baking soda dissolved in
>   ¼ cup hot water
>   Brandy, Sherry, or Whisky Sauce (page 87)

Mix all ingredients together, adding the dissolved baking soda last. Put into a buttered mould and steam (see page 78) for 3 hours. Serve hot with Brandy, Sherry, or Whisky Sauce.

BLAUMA PUDDING
(Plum Pudding)

Here's one made with plums.

>   1⅓ cups flour
>   2 teaspoons baking soda
>   ½ teaspoon salt
>   ¼ teaspoon allspice
>   ¼ teaspoon nutmeg
>   2 cups stoned plums, cut in half
>   1 tablespoon melted shortening

¼ cup honey
⅓ cup hot water
Grated rind of 1 lemon
Brown Sugar Sauce (page 85)

Sift the dry ingredients and add the plums. Combine the shortening, honey, hot water, and lemon rind and add to first mixture, blending well. Pour the batter into a well-greased mould, cover and steam (see page 78) for 2½ hours. Unmould and serve hot with sauce.

CLARA MAY'S STEAMED BREAD PUDDING

The Ingraham family was always glad when there was enough bread left from last week's baking to make this great pudding.

2 cups dried bread
¼ cup white or brown sugar
1 egg
3 tablespoons shortening
½ teaspoon baking soda
1 cup molasses
1 cup raisins
Lemon or vanilla or rum flavouring
1 teaspoon cinnamon
½ teaspoon ginger
About 1 cup flour
Brown Sugar Sauce (page 85)

Moisten the bread with water then squeeze it out till it's almost dry, rub it together with your hands till there are no lumps, Clara May told me. Add all the other ingredients and finally about 1 cup of flour till the mixture is like a cake batter. Steam for about 1½ hours (see page 78). Serve with Brown Sugar Sauce flavoured with rum. No wonder this was Henry's favourite puddin'.

STEAMED JAM OR MARMALADE PUDDING

A good way to get rid of that jam in the bottom of the jar.

> 2 tablespoons shortening
> ¼ cup sugar
> 1 egg, beaten
> 6 tablespoons jam or marmalade
> 1½ cups flour
> 1 tablespoon baking powder
> ½ teaspoon salt
> 1 tablespoon milk
> Brown Sugar or Brandy Sauce (page 85 or 87)

Cream shortening and add sugar. Add egg and jam. Sift flour, baking powder and salt into the mixture. Add milk if needed to moisten. Put in mould or bowl and steam for 2½ hours. Serve hot with Brown Sugar or Brandy Sauce.

ST. JAMES PUDDING

> 3 tablespoons butter, melted
> ½ cup bran
> ½ cup molasses
> ½ cup buttermilk
> 1½ cups flour
> ½ teaspoon baking soda
> ½ teaspoon salt
> ¼ teaspoon each of cloves, allspice, and nutmeg
> 1 cup dates, cut in pieces

Combine butter, bran, molasses, and milk. Sift flour, baking soda, salt, and spices; add to first mixture, with dates, stirring only until combined. Fill greased mould about ⅔ full. Cover tightly and steam 3 hours. Serve hot with sauce.

BLUEBERRY MUSH

This can also be made with other berries, apples, or peaches.

> 2 cups flour
> 4 teaspoons baking powder
> 1 teaspoon salt
> 1 tablespoon butter
> ¾ cup milk
> 2 cups sugar
> 4 cups berries
> 1 teaspoon lemon juice
> Cream, plain or whipped

Sift flour, baking powder, and salt together and work in the butter. Add the milk and blend thoroughly. Combine the sugar, berries, and lemon juice. Mix with batter. Pour into a buttered mould, cover tightly and steam for 45 minutes. Serve with plain or whipped cream.

LOTTIE RITTINGER'S SNOW BALLS

You don't need an ever-burning wood stove to make this.

> ¼ cup butter
> ½ cup sugar
> ¼ cup milk
> 1⅛ cups flour
> 2 teaspoons baking powder
> 2 egg whites
> Chocolate Sauce (page 86)

Cream butter and sugar, stir in the milk and beat until sugar is dissolved. Sift in flour and baking powder, and beat thoroughly. Fold in the beaten egg whites. Put into buttered moulds and steam 35 minutes. Serve with Chocolate Sauce.

DESSERT SAUCES

These dessert sauces will enhance any pudding. A slightly old cake can be heated and freshened and made special with a sauce that complements its flavour. A dessert sauce can mask almost any failure — don't tell that it wasn't intended. And poured over ice cream, what could be better?

BUTTERSCOTCH SAUCE

1 cup brown sugar
2 tablespoons cornstarch
⅛ teaspoon salt
2 tablespoons butter
4 teaspoons water
1 cup cold water
1 teaspoon vanilla or rum flavouring or
   3 to 4 tablespoons rum or brandy

Combine the sugar, cornstarch, salt, butter, and 2 dessertspoons water in a saucepan over heat; stir until the mixture melts and turns brown. Add 1 cup cold water, cook till it thickens. Remove from heat, add flavouring. It's even very good without rum.

MOTHER'S BUTTERSCOTCH SAUCE

Mother writes in her little black book, "This is very good, even on cake."

1½ cups brown sugar
½ cup corn syrup
4 tablespoons butter
½ cup cream
1 teaspoon vanilla

Bring sugar, syrup, and butter to a boil and cook until soft ball forms when a bit is dropped in cold water. Remove from heat and cool. When cold, add cream and vanilla.

BROWN SUGAR SAUCE I

1½ cups brown sugar
2 cups boiling water
4 tablespoons butter

Boil all together for about 10 minutes.

BROWN SUGAR SAUCE II

2 tablespoons butter
3 tablespoons flour or
   1½ tablespoons cornstarch
1 cup brown sugar
2 cups boiling water
1 teaspoon vanilla

Melt the butter, add the flour and stir until smooth. Add the sugar, keep stirring and cook until it becomes a darker brown. Slowly add the water and cook until thick, then add vanilla.

CUSTARD SAUCE

Whenever you make something that uses egg whites and not yolks, you could use the yolks to make this schmecksy, easy, and useful custard sauce. It is a booster for many puddings and an essential with Lemon Snow.

1 cup milk
2 egg yolks
3 tablespoons sugar
Pinch of salt
½ teaspoon vanilla or almond flavouring

In a double boiler, scald the milk. In a bowl, beat egg yolks. Add sugar and salt and beat until light. Pour scalded milk over mixture, blend, and return to double boiler. Cook till sauce coats a wooden spoon, stirring constantly. Chill and add vanilla.

THIN CHOCOLATE SAUCE

Or for a milk drink. This is not thick or rich — but delicious on ice cream.

　　1¾ cups water
　　1 cup cocoa
　　1½ cups sugar (white or brown)
　　½ teaspoon salt

Stir all together and boil 5 minutes. Keep in a sealed container in a cool place. Serve hot or cold on ice cream — or add 1 tablespoon to a cup or glass of hot or cold milk.

CHOCOLATE SAUCE

　　2 squares unsweetened chocolate
　　　(or ½ cup cocoa)
　　1 cup hot water
　　1 tablespoon cornstarch
　　1 cup sugar
　　¼ teaspoon salt
　　1 tablespoon butter
　　1 teaspoon vanilla

Melt chocolate in top part of double boiler. Gradually add hot water and stir until smooth. Dissolve cornstarch in a little cold water and add to chocolate mixture with sugar and salt; stir frequently until mixture is thick and smooth — about 10 minutes. Remove from heat and add butter and vanilla.

FUDGE SAUCE — HOT OR COLD

Is there anything better than hot fudge sauce on ice cream? We used to go to the Busy Bee every night after school for a Hot Fudge Sundae with toasted almonds — until they raised the price to 15 cents. Miserable day!

　　½ cup cocoa
　　1 cup sugar

1 cup corn syrup
½ cup milk
2 to 4 tablespoons butter
¼ teaspoon salt
1 teaspoon vanilla

Put everything but the vanilla in a saucepan and cook over medium heat, stirring all the time; bring to a full rolling boil and let it go for 3 minutes. Take from the heat and add the vanilla. Serve hot for a more fudgy flavour.

Store it in the fridge with a lid that's hard to get off. It will thicken but can be thinned for pouring by placing in a pan of hot water. It won't last long.

NORM'S SHERRY SAUCE

½ cup sugar
1 tablespoon cornstarch
Pinch of salt
1 cup boiling water
2 tablespoons butter
1 tablespoon vanilla
1 jigger sweet sherry

Mix sugar, cornstarch, salt; add water gradually, stirring constantly as you boil it for 5 minutes. Remove from heat; add butter, vanilla, and wine.

RUBY'S BRANDY, WHISKY, OR SHERRY SAUCE

1½ tablespoons cornstarch
½ cup sugar
¼ teaspoon salt
1 cup hot water
Juice and grated rind of 1 lemon
1 tablespoon butter
½ cup brandy (or whisky or sherry)

Combine cornstarch, sugar, and salt, add water, grated lemon rind and juice; cook gently, stirring constantly until thick and clear. Add butter and sherry. Serve hot.

RUM-BUTTER SAUCE

This is dreamy over ice cream or pudding.

> 2 tablespoons cornstarch — or clearjell
> ½ teaspoon salt
> 1 cup sugar
> 2 cups boiling water
> 2 tablespoons butter
> 1 ounce rum
> Juice of ½ lemon

In a saucepan, combine cornstarch, salt, and sugar. Add boiling water gradually, stirring constantly. Bring to a boil, stirring for 5 minutes. Remove from heat, then add butter, rum, and lemon juice.

MALLOW MINT SAUCE

> ½ cup sugar
> ⅓ cup water
> ⅛ teaspoon cream of tartar
> 8 marshmallows, cut in pieces
> Few frops peppermint

Boil the sugar and water for 3 minutes. Add cream of tartar. Put in the marshmallows. Stir until smooth, then flavour with peppermint. Pour over the chocolate mountains (page 55). Double the recipe if you like more.

LEMON SAUCE

½ cup sugar
¼ teaspoon salt
1½ tablespoons cornstarch
1½ cups boiling water
2 tablespoons butter
Grated rind and juice of 1 lemon

Combine sugar, salt, and cornstarch. Slowly add the water and cook in a double boiler until mixture thickens and is clear, stirring constantly. Remove from heat and stir in the butter until melted, then stir in the grated lemon rind and juice until well blended.

The juice and rind of an orange could be used if you want Orange Sauce.

CARROT OR PLUM-PUDDING SAUCE

1 cup brown sugar
2 tablespoons cornstarch
½ teaspoon salt
2 cups boiling water
¼ cup butter
2 jiggers of sweet wine, brandy, whisky or rum
— or 2 teaspoons vanilla

Mix sugar, cornstarch, salt; add water gradually, stirring, constantly. Boil for 5 minutes — till thickened and clear; remove from heat, add butter; let it melt as you stir, then add liquor or vanilla.

RUM OR BRANDY HARD SAUCE

Take equal quantities of **softened butter** or **icing sugar** and beat thoroughly together. Slowly beat in **brandy or rum**, a few drops at a time. When you can mix in no more without it separating, put it in the refrigerator to harden and serve with hot Christmas pudding.

INDEX

Apple
  Betty, 12
  Crownest, 8
  Dumplings, 4
  Fruity Pudding, 10
  Hasty Pudding, 9
  Oatmeal Squares, 5
  Pancake (Pfannkuchen), 6
  Sauce, 3
  Speedy Nut Pudding, 11
  Sponge Pudding, 10
  Strudel, 7
  in Winter Fruit, 20
Banana
  Baked in Rum, 37
  Ice, 73
  with Pavlova, 40
  Prune Whip, 38
  Split, 75
  Sponge, 66
  in Winter Fruit, 20
Blueberry Mush, 83
Bread Puddings
  Clara May's, steamed, 81
  Hunter's, 59
  Mother's, 58
  New Orleans, 60
Carrot Pudding, 80
Cheesecake, 46
Cherry Betty, 14
Chocolate or Cocoa
  Banana Split, 75
  Custard, 47
  Dessert, 51
  Devil's Food, 45
  Fudge Sauce, 86
  Marshmallow Ice Cream, 68
  Mint Mousse, 48
  Mocha Nut Tortoni, 74

Mocha Rum Mousse, 48
Mocha Torte, 43
Pot de Crème, 49
Prune Whip, 66
Rice Pudding, 53
Sauce, 86
Snow on the Mountain, 55
Soufflé, 39
Tapioca, 54
Wafer Dessert, 49
Cobblers
  Plum, 33
  Rhubarb, 25
  Spicy Rhubarb, 25
  Strawberry Rhubarb, 25
Coffee
  Caramel Ice Cream, 70
  Grand Marnier Café, 64
  Jelly, 66
  Mocha Rum Mousse, 48
  Mocha Torte, 43
  Mocha Nut Tortoni, 74
  Pot de Crème Chocolat, 49
  Prune Whip, 66
Custard
  Baked, 47
  Chocolate, 47
  Maple, 47
  Rhubarb, 28
  Sauce, 85
Dumplings
  Apple, 4
  Plum, 35
  Twenty-Minute, 57
Eggnog, Quivering, 65
Fruit (dried)
  Babas au Rhum, 42
  Bread Pudding (Clara May's), 81

INDEX

Bread Pudding (New Orleans), 60
Carrot Pudding, 80
Christmas Plum Pudding, 78
Creamy Rice, 52
English Christmas Pudding, 79
Fruit Batter Pudding, 22
Jell-o Pudding, 63
Quick Pudding, 57
Spicy, 21
St. James Pudding, 82
Fruit (fresh)
  Batter Pudding, 22
  Jell-o, 63
  Pavlova, 40
  Roll, 16
  Watermelon Boat, 21
  Winter, 20
Ice Cream
  Banana Split, 75
  Coffee Caramel, 70
  Cranberry, 71
  Easy, 69
  Ginger, 70
  Marshmallow-Cocoa, 68
  Mint Parfait, 71
  Mocha Nut Tortoni, 74
  Quick Crispie Dessert, 76
  Sauce, 45
  Strawberries Québécois, 76
  Vanilla, 69
Lemon
  Citrus Soufflé, 61
  Delight, 64
  Foam, 38
  Sauce, 89
  Snow, 62
  Soufflé, 46
  Strawberries and Wine, 19

Syllabub, 39
Water Ice, 73
Maple
  Custard, 47
  Mousse, 62
  Pudding, 59
  Rice Pudding, 54
Meringues
  Mocha Nut Tortoni, 74
  Pavlova, 40
  Peach Pie, 15
  Perfect, 41
  Rhubarb Custard, 28
Mince Meat Rolls, 16
Mint
  Chocolate Mousse, 48
  Marshmallow Sauce, 88
  Parfait, 71
Mousse
  Chocolate Mint, 48
  Maple, 62
  Mocha Rum, 48
Peach
  Meringue Pie, 15
  with Pavlova, 40
  Sherbet, 74
  Shortcake, 13
Pear
  Flaming Melba, 17
Pineapple
  with Pavlova, 40
  in Watermelon Boat, 21
  in Winter Fruit, 20
Plum
  Blauma Pudding, 80
  Cobbler, 33
  Crumble, 34
  Dumplings, 35
  Fool, 34
  Party Cake, 31
  Pudding, 32, 78, 79

INDEX

Stewed, 33
Prune
  Banana Whip, 38
  with Dried Fruit, 21
  New Orleans Whip, 66
  Whip, 20
Raspberry
  Banana Split, 75
  Flaming Pear Melba, 17
  Pudding, 18
Rhubarb
  Baked, 26
  Cobbler, 25
  Crisp, 27
  Crunch, 24
  Custard Meringue, 28
  Dream, 26
  Roll, 20
  Spicy Cobbler, 25
  Stewed, 27
  Strawberry Cobbler, 25
  Strawberry Roll, 29
  Turnovers, 29
Rum
  Babas, 42
  Baked Bananas, 37
  in Bread Pudding, 60
  Butter Sauce, 88
  Carrot Pudding Sauce, 89
  Hard Sauce, 89
  Hot Sauce, 42
  Mocha Mousse, 48
  Plum Pudding Sauce, 89
  in Quivering Eggnog, 65
  in Trifle, 44
Sauces
  Brandy, Whisky and
    Sherry, 87
  Brown Sugar #1, 85
  Brown Sugar #2, 85
  Butterscotch, 84
  Butterscotch (Mother's), 84
  Carrot or Plum-Pudding, 89
  Chocolate, 86
  Custard, 85
  Fudge, 86
  Hot Rum, 42
  Ice-Cream, 45
  Mallow Mint, 88
  Rum or Brandy Hard, 89
  Rum-Butter, 88
  Sherry, 87
Soufflés
  Chocolate, 39
  Citrus, 61
  Lemon, 46
  Sherry, 63
Strawberry
  Banana Split, 75
  Delight, 72
  with Lemon and Wine, 19
  Meringues, 41
  with Pavlova, 40
  Québécois, 76
  Rhubarb Cobbler, 25
  Rhubarb Roll, 29
  Shortcake, 13
  Snow, 67
  in Watermelon Boat, 21
Syllabub, 50
  Lemon, 39
Tapioca, 54
  Chocolate, 54
Trifle, 44
Wafer Dessert
  Chocolate, 49
  Ginger, 49
Watermelon Boat, 21